LOVE BANK

Covenant Love

Author Aneesah Perkins

Editor Debbie Guzman

And Laura Alhomsi

Contents

Unless otherwise indicated, all scripture quotations are from the Holy Bible, New International Version ®, NIV ®, © 1973, 1978, 1984 BY THE INTERNATIONAL BIBLE SOCIETY. All rights reserved. All Scripture quotations marked (KJV) are from the New King James Version of the Holy Bible.

First Printing: 2013

ISBN 978-1-304-35671-0

ISBN 978-1-312-92143-6

Mahogany Brides Magazine L.L.C
P.O. BOX 1134
Edmond, Oklahoma 73083

E-MAIL maghoganybrides@gmail.com

Website: www.mahoganybridesmagazine.weebly.com

E-MAIL authoraneesahperkins@gmail.com

Website: www.lovebank.weebly.com

Dedication

To my lovely husband Delano McCoy, my wonderful Children, my editor Debbie Guzman-Conner, and Love Bank's TV Series Cast.

Thank you. Without your support and patience, I would have never achieved my dream.

It is an honor to have my Husband right beside me, to help and support my vision and mission for today's men and women of Christ. Love Bank was written to help other men and women know the value of being in the body of Christ.

To my beloved Children: to whom I have dedicated my life of being a great mother and mentor to. It is a blessing to have healthy, smart and beautiful children. Thank you, God.

To my lovely editor: Debbie Guzman-Conner to whom I honor and adore for having such patience and love for me and my work. Thank you for believing and working with me. A woman of substance and integrity; who has never stopped believing in me.

Acknowledgements

Every accomplishment in my life has truly been a blessing from God. Contributions from friends and family members have helped me grow and overcome many obstacles in my life. It is an honor and a blessing for me to have friends with gifts, talents and wisdom. My husband Delano McCoy was not only my husband but a true friend, who valued my talents and dreams. Without the love, support and prayers from my family and friends I would have not been able to publish Love Bank.

I want to thank everyone at Mahogany Brides Magazine L.L.C. for their never wavering support and dedication in helping to publish Love Bank's book. Thank you to all the Mahogany Brides Magazine staff members and models.

I appreciate all of the men and women who follow and support Love Bank's book, play, and TV series. It has been a blessing to meet and greet everyone. May God bless you and keep you in my prayers.

Introduction

Men and women are extremely different but also very alike in many ways. Men and women have the same requirements when it comes to love, attention and affection. Quality women in the twenty-first century require real authentic love rather than a roller coaster love or relationship. Men in the twenty-first century require their options. Either a man will treat you or he will trick you. Men will let you know up front in their conversation or body language. As a woman, one must know what she is getting herself into and decided what type of relationship she wants. Women around the world are facing an identity crisis. Many women are struggling to discover who they are and what they were put on this earth to do rather than just have children. The roles for women are forever changing in family, the community, and the world. Women's personal expectations are changing due to the role that has been given to them by man, because of their lack of leadership and stand in the world. However, there has also been a twist in man's role too. Now in the twenty-first century a man is willing to sit home and watch the kids and take care of the home while the wife makes all the money for the household. There has been a major change in expectations and roles in life for men and women. Men have also taken a step down to be happy and to be loved by independent, strong, and beautiful women. Questions at times enter my mind and I ask: 1.) How do we as people change the roles back to God's will? 2.) Do we as people keep the new changes of men and women's roles of the twenty-first century? The question of a man's or woman's status role is no longer a secret or issues. Equal rights are a given and are required for high levels of leadership in the United States and most parts of the world. Love Bank was written to express the true aspects of the man being the leader and comforter in the marriage. Men and women will also see how important it is to allow the man to lead and the woman to follow, as God's perfect will and purpose for ordained marriages and relationships. Love Bank the Covenant Love. Leadership that was given to man and woman by the son of God, Father and the Holy Spirit is expressed and is fulfilled.

Chapter 1
Talking in my Sleep

A room adorned with luxury furniture and tall royal swag curtains embellished Karen Matthew's gold accented room. The smell of fresh flowers filled Karen's room; these were left daily by her Colombian maid Emma. Still at the age of 35 Karen's father, Mr. Matthews, has his only daughter believing that she is the only princess in the world. Karen was taught at an early age by her mother, Mrs. Matthews, to have matching pajamas, look beautiful, and to have gorgeous hair at all times because her prince charming could show up at any moment and rescue her. Karen laid restless tossing and turning while dreaming in her satin purple sheets. She sees herself dancing with an unknown man. The unknown man looks very handsome. Karen is very excited because he has all his teeth. Karen loves a man with a great smile and who has all his teeth. The two of them were all dressed in white clothing. Karen could tell that they knew each other, but from where she does not know. Karen and the handsome unknown man danced endlessly in love, hand in hand; and then all of a sudden, they are separated. Karen tries to reach out and grab his hand in the dark, but only grasps the air. Karen realizes it's too late and the unknown man disappears. God's sweet scent God's sweet scent perfumes her room with his holy presence. Karen lifts up her buried head from all her 10 pillows lying on her bed. Karen believed as a little girl that all queens and princesses should sleep with nice quality pillows and sit high while asleep. Karen turns over and sits up in her queen sized bed and blinks twice as she pulls her long black shoulder length hair out of her face and eyes as she begins to cry while sitting up in her bed. The voice of the Lord speaks out and says, ''Karen why are you crying?'' Karen replies back and says, ''Lord is that you?'' The Lord replies back and says, "Yes, I am the Lord of all.'' Karen replies back, ''Oh it's you Lord....Hello, Lord. I'm crying because I am tired of being all alone Lord. Where is my husband...? My help mate Lord?" The Lord Replies back and says, "Karen do you trust me?" Karen replies and says, "Why yes Lord. I trust you with all my heart." The Lord replies and says, "Then go and read the book of Genesis and I will heal your broken heart. I will bless you with a mate. Prepare to get married this year." Karen's eyes get big and she pinches herself and says to the Lord, "Is he handsome Lord? Does he have all his teeth? Does he have a nice smile?" The Lord laughs as he replies and says, "Karen he has all those things and more." Karen's eyes began to roam her room and she begins to cover her face with her hands because of her excitement. Everything that has been in her heart about her husband was place by the Holy Spirit. Karen speaks out with a loud voice again and says, "Lord you remember what I asked for in my mate!" Karen begins to cry tears of joy. Karen replies and says, "But wait Lord, how will I know if he is the one? So many men have walked before me Lord." The Lord replies and says, "You will know him by his fruit." Karen replies back, "Wow, you mean he will be wearing fruit Lord." The Lord laughs and says, "Karen, my beloved daughter, the man I have for you will be wearing the fruits of my spirit." Karen replies back and says, "Oh, Lord! I thought for a moment he would be wearing actual fruit." Karen begins to laugh at herself. The Lord says to Karen, "Rest my beloved and remember to trust me for I am the Lord of all. (Psalm 56:4) Remember

to read the book of Psalms."

Karen moves to the right side edge of her bed and is grinning from cheek to cheek. While sitting for a moment Karen is in awe and is allowing everything to sink in. As Karen is sitting she begins touching her sheets, covers, and her pajamas. Karen notices that the sheets, covers, and pajamas are real. To make sure she is not dreaming she stands up and pinches herself. She says yelp "I am fully awake...I was really talking to God." Karen begins to cry again, but they are tears of joy. Wiping away her tears, Karen stands with confidence. Karen notices that she received boldness and clarity from the Lord. Karen gets out of bed and lifts her right hand to worship the Lord and begins to speak out the words, "Thank you Lord for your love and your word fulfilling me." Karen is excited about the good news and the presence of the Lord. Karen begins to focus and get ready to walk into her bathroom but suddenly changes her mind and goes the opposite direction of her bathroom. Karen notices a family portrait of her mother and father and walks over to the photo. Remembering what the Lord told her about her mate Karen begins to touch her clothes again and starts to smile while dancing across her room. Karen suddenly stops in midair and looks up at her clock on the wall and says, "Oh my gosh! It is almost time for me to go to work." Karen rushes into her bathroom and turns on the lights and begins to stare at herself smile in the mirror. She looks up to the ceiling while lifting her right hand to God and begins to praise him for his glory and begins to hum a melody. Karen finally humbles herself to sit down on her specially made praying bench, where she prays every morning before she starts her day. Karen begins to speak out and say, "God as I come boldly before your throne, I want to say thank you for your never ending love and blessings you have bestowed on my life. I thank you for my family. It is an honor and a privilege to know you and bless your holy and mighty name. Lord I thank you for your word that does not come back unto you void. I also thank you for proving day in and day out to be true in my life. Lord I pray for everyone in my life in and around my life. I pray that all their needs are met and that every tongue that rises up against me and shall be condemned and shall be moved. In Jesus name Amen. I seal it and declare it in Jesus name I pray. Amen. Thank you in advance Lord for your blessings today." Karen gets up from her prayer bench and begins to take off her clothes. While choosing her towel Karen stops her focus on the towels and reaches over to cut on the water in her shower and then grabs a towel and jumps into the shower. The Lord comes to her again while in the shower and says, "Rejoice in the Lord for this is the day I have made. Blessings and challenges are coming your way. Fret not. Karen, know that I will never leave you or forsake you." Karen begins to smile and lift both of her hands in worship and cry out to the Lord again for his goodness and mercy. Karen begins to wash her body and hair and then touches her stomach and graces over her belly button and imagines she is pregnant. Karen loves kids. The warm water was only touching parts of her body; so, she begins to grab water with both of her hands and throws the water onto her face and body. As Karen skin drinks the water, the water begins to bring Karen into reality of the natural world around her and she finishes her shower. Without a doubt Karen believes and trusts in the Lord, but he does not know what's to come, and does not know when or how it will turn out. Karen turns off the water and grabs her soft Turkish monogrammed. As she steps out onto her soft patterned rug she begins to dry off and blots her long hair. The scent of Christ still fills Karen's room and she smiles and begins to get dressed. All of a sudden Karen hears a knock on her bathroom door and she already knows who it could be, no one but her maid Emma. There's another knock at the door so then Karen feels that maybe it's not Emma. Emma would have said something by then. Karen finishes putting on all her clothes and she opens the door and she sees no one. Karen looks around the room and all of a sudden Karen's eyes stumble up on her ex-lover NBA player Rodney. Karen gasps for air as she tries to cover up her smile, while looking big eyed at Rodney. Rodney looks right back at Karen showing off all his perfect teeth and smile on his face. Karen looks Rodney from head to toe and notices Rodney is holding a dozen of pink roses wrapped in clear plastic along with a red satin ribbon in his hand. Karen tries to gain her posture back and get firm and says to Rodney, "Who let you in? Wait a minute, don't answer that." Karen takes her eyes off of Rodney and begins to yell for her maid, " Emma....Emma." Karen turns her head and looks at Rodney and directs her attention back onto Rodney. Rodney replies back and says, "I'm sorry if I startled you Karen. I thought I'd come by and say hello to you. I have been thinking about you and missing you. You have been on my mind so I decided to come by this morning to see you." Karen looks at Rodney and says, "You what...Did you just say you missed me, since when Rodney?" Rodney is slow to speak and smiles and says, ''Karen I have always loved you and thought of you. It's just that....It's just that I have a career that is very demanding and I am sorry that I haven't been the best fiancé or boyfriend in the world to you. I am here now and I want to let you know that I love you and I want us back again.'' Karen looks at Rodney with a very intense stare, as if she could kill him with her eyes and with an attitude of I've heard it all before look. Karen begins to speak with boldness in her in voice and says, ''Rodney, really let's be honest and explain to me why are you really here right now in my home and how did you get into my neighborhood? You know I live in a gated community as you can see and they just don't let anyone in here.'' Looking right into Karen's eyes Rodney says, ''Ah yes, you're lovely maid Emma let me in.'' Rodney's face is beaming with laughter as and he says, ''I told her I wanted to surprise you and not to bother you and If she could go and get things for you and I later.'' Karen looks at him and says '' later Rodney, really? What do you mean later, there is no later for us. What do you have up your sleeve? Rodney begins to say ''well I thought you and I could have a candlelight romantic dinner tonight. Karen says '' you did what?, oh you have got some nerve to come in here and think that everything is okay after all these years of you being out of my life.'' Rodney you are going to show up and try to smooth things over with some fancy expensive roses?'' Rodney butts in while Karen is going off on a tantrum and says Karen in reality you left me...I never left you. Karen's eyes get big and she looks at Rodney while he is still speaking and says ''oh really. So what do you call having 2 other non speaking English want to be wife material women by your side?'' Rodney says ''ah Karen they were just groupies, they did not mean nothing to me." Karen tries to stand her ground and not to walk away but he says to Rodney "then why didn't you make them go away. And If I was really what you wanted then why did you not prove it to me. You left me on the sideline many of times. I remember those days like they were yesterday. I waited for you to come out of your locker room many of times but you never came. Somehow, someway you always got passed me." So again, why are you here? Let me guess you must have fell and bumped your big head and realized, that if you did not get your life right that you will be by yourself. Rodney smile and laughs. Rodney says somewhat true but not all but " you know Karen I actually miss you calling me big head." Rodney walks over to Karen and tries to reach for her but Karen pulls her hand back and Rodney says "can I hold your hand?" Karen looks at Rodney and says " who, what.... awe naw potna, but you can get out of here. The devil is a lie....You are not my husband." Rodney looks stunned and says "hey, how did you know I was coming over to propose to you tonight Karen?" Karen's mouth drops open and she loses her breath, faints and falls to the floor. Rodney tries to catch Karen from falling but misses. her fall. Rodney rushes to Karen and drops to the floor and picks up Karen's head and body while checking her pulse and say's " Please don't die on me Karen....I am a changed man. I promise to do right by you/" Rodney bends over to kiss Karen on her forehead and then he begins to lift Karen' body up and walks her over to her bed and puts her inside of her queen size bed. Rodney reaches for his cell phone while his hands are trembling to get in the inside of his suit coat jacket. Rodney finally gets his cell phone out and begins to dial 911. Rodney is very stunned and shocked and don't know what to do. The operator from 911 picks up and Rodney begins to describe what happened to Karen and is told by the 911 operator that the police will be on their way. Rodney makes another call to Karen's parents and hopes that they do not hang up on him. Mr. Matthews picks up and answers the call. Rodney blurts out all at once and tells him to hurry and come over to Karen's house. Mr. and Mrs. Mathews tell Rodney that they are on their way. Rodney begins to hear footsteps walking up to Karen's room. The door opens and it's Emma. Emma sees Karen on the floor and her mouth drops. Emma, without thinking reaches back into her cleaning basket and grabs her broom and starts to charge at Rodney while yelling and talking in her native language. Rodney begins to yell back and say please Emma this is not what it looks like. Emma is still swing at Rodney while crying and still talking in her native language. Rodney begins yell out and say 'please Emma I don't know what you are saying, please speak English if you can. I can't understand you Emma. Emma starts talking in English " you killed Karen....Now I'm going to kill you. You, you low down dirty creep." "I have should've never let you in. You are going to pay for this." "Rodney's eyes gets big and yells out please...please Emma it's not what you think. Please believe me...I did not kill Karen. Karen fainted when I asked her for her hand in marriage. Emma stops the broom in mid air and stares at Rodney. Rodney blinks and then smiles at Emma and says "yes, yes I have trying to tell you this." Emma replies back and says" Yeah right! I don't believe you. I find it very hard to believe that you would ask Karen to marry you." " I am going to get you, you two timing want to be NBA playa." "I 'am going teach you about being a playa, playa." Rodney begins to duck and move from side to side and around the room while yelling out " Please Emma I am telling you the truth. I did not do anything to Karen she just fainted after I told her I wanted to marry her." Emma suddenly stops and gains her balance and smiles at Rodney and says "Oh my gosh! Rodney are you really wanting to marry Karen?" Emma walks over to Rodney and shakes his hand and" says congratulations" I am very sorry for trying to kill you. Rodney wipes off his forehead and then wipes his hand on his pants then shakes Emma' hand. Rodney then tells Emma the ambulance on its way. Rodney begins to peek out and tell Emma "Yes, I really do love her and I want to marry her. Please help me. I have already called the police." The police burst into the room with the paramedics and they put Karen onto the stretcher bed and check to see if she is still breathing. The police come over to Rodney and start asking him for his name and for his Id. Karen's parents come through the door and rush over to Karen and asks Rodney if she will be okay. Rodney nodes to them and says " yes, Karen will be fine she just fainted." One of the paramedics began to say we just got here but we are sure she will be fine we are going to do everything we can. Mr. Matthews walks over to Rodney and ask him what caused Karen to faint. Rodney answers Mr. Mathews question while Rodney looks over and sees Emma praying over Karen's body while holding her hand. Karen's mother is crying. Mrs. Mathews says my baby, my only baby girl. God please let her live don't take her away from me." Mr. Matthews walks over to Mrs. Mathew's side and tries to comfort his wife by trying to hug her. Mrs. Mathews hugs him back. Karen makes a sudden move and then she wakes up and opens her eyes. The paramedics began to shout to everyone that her eyes are opening, so let's get her down stairs and stable. The police tell Rodney that they will be asking more questions at the hospital so don't go far. Everyone starts clearing out of Karen's room and goes down stairs. Karen gets placed into the ambulance and taken to the hospital. Mr. & Mrs. Mathews tell Emma that she can ride with them. Rodney tells them that he is going to drive his own car. A police officer comes back into the room and asks to speak to Karen's mom. The police officer asks to speak with her for a moment and says I promise I won't keep you long but I have some information about your daughter. The Mathews step to the side with the police officer and answer the questions. Emma walks out the door and prepare to gather her things for the ride. The paramedics get Karen stable and they drive off rushing to the hospital. Emma is in tears while praying with her rosary red bead necklace around her hand, she suddenly looks up and kisses her fingers as to say thank you God. Rodney arrives at the hospital and he sees Emma sitting down with her eyes being closed. The nurses take Karen back to her room and check her into the hospital. The Mathews go back with the nurse and ask to speak to the Dr. who is on duty. The nurse explains that the Dr. that is on duty is named Dr. White. Dr. White comes over to Karen's parents and says hello, I believe we have met before. The Mathews smile and say yes, it's been a long time, it's good to see you again. Both parents are asked by Dr. White to come and speak to him about Karen's fall. Mr. Mathews begins to tell Dr. White what had happened. The Dr. replies back and says " I am sorry but when your daughter hit her head on the mahogany wooden floors, it caused her to have a little scar tissue. Mrs. Mathews says Dr. White with all due respect please get to the point. What are you trying to tell us. Mr. Mathews say's "please Yvonne....let the man speak, so we both can see what's wrong with our daughter." Dr. White smiles and says "Thank you Mr. Mathew as I was saying, Karen has had a big blow to her head and we want to keep her in the hospital for a few days and run some tests on her to make sure everything checks out okay. Perhaps if everything checks out okay then she can be released to go home. Rodney slips up and butts into the conversation and says," you mean she has to stay here for a couple of days? Man, ain't nobody got time for this. I have a game in less than two days." Dr. White says "I am sorry and you are?" Mrs. Mathews butts in and says" ah nobody important please keep talking." Mr. Mathews assures that it is okay to keep talking with Rodney around. Dr. White says "ah yes back to what I was saying that it will be in your best interest that you allow her to stay here for a couple of days." Dr. White walks away. Rodney begins to say to Mrs. Mathews and Mr. Mathews "with all due respect I would like to marry your daughter Karen." Mr. Mathews steps back and looks at Rodney and say's since when? I have not heard of you or this, Yvonne who is this and why don't i know him? I don't even know you and yet you ask for my daughter's hand in marriage. Wait a minute son come again, what did you just say?" Rodney gets a little nervous and tries to stand up straight and says "yes sir, this is correct I was wanting to ask for your daughter's hand in marriage this afternoon but Karen fainted before I could come and ask you for your daughter's hand in marriage."

Rodney goes on to say "you see Mr. Matthews I was going to ask your daughter to marry me tonight over a nice romantic candlelight dinner, but it does not look like it is going to happen right now". Mr. Mathews comes over to

Rodney and shakes his hand and hugs him and says" thank you but you are not in with me just yet." Mrs. Matthews looks at Mr. Mathews and looks at Rodney with disappointment and says "God still has the last word. Over my dead body will I ever allow you to marry my daughter." Mrs. Matthews walks away and Mr. Matthews tries to follow his wife but feels that she does not want to be bothered. Mrs. Matthews walks into Karen's room. Rodney can tell that Karen's mom is not too happy with him and hopes that she understands that he is a changed man. Rodney begins to say "I was not the best person to your daughter." Rodney puts his head down and his right hand begins to rub his forehead and his eyes look from side to side. Rodney begins to shed a tear and sits down. Mr. Matthews walks into Karen's room and sees Mrs. Matthew sitting down by Karen's bed. Mrs. Matthews is looking at Karen sleeping in the bed. Karen's mom begins to cry out to the Lord and asks him to come and heal Karen's head and body so that she can return home. Karen opens her eyes and then turns her head and sees her mom crying. Mr. Mathews rushes over to the bed and begins to grace his daughter's head and says " how is my little princess? Karen smiles back at her father and says " I am doing fine dad. Mrs. Mathews wipes her tears and tells Karen that she loves her and that everything is going to be okay." Karen looks around the room and asks how she got in the hospital. Mr. Mathews begin to explain what happened to her and tell her not to try to talk too much. Mr. Mathews tells Karen that she must take it easy. Karen raised her head and she reaches to the side of her head and rubs over her lump on the side of her head and begins to cry. Mrs. Mathews says to Karen" No sweetheart you are going to be fine it's not as bad as you think." Mrs. Mathews begin to explain again that the Dr. says that she will be out of here in no time." Karen asks how did she get here again and asks who called 911 to help her out of her home. Mrs. Mathews says Karen let's focus on something else right now. You should be hungry right now, let me go see if Dr. White will allow you to eat anything right now. I will be right back. Karen says" okay but you promise to tell me what's wrong and how did I get here today mom? Mrs. Mathews says " I promise princess, I will tell you everything." Karen lays her head back onto the pillow and Mrs. Matthew leaves the room and Rodney slips through the door and say " hello Karen…how are you doing? How is my Wife to be. Karen raises her head from the pillow and looks directly at Rodney and frowns and says what are you doing here? Rodney comes closer to the bed and gives Karen a kiss on the forehead and gives her a hug. Karen I love you so much… I am so glad I still have you in my life. You scared me. I thought I was never going to see you again. You are a really strong woman and I am blessed to have you in my life. I came by to your house today to ask you to marry me." Karen's mouth drops open and then covers her mouth and says "me marry you Rodney? I am hurt but I am not that hurt. Rodney asks Karen if she would please marry him. I will marry you on one condition" and Rodney answers back and says and that is? If you ever cheat or have disrespectful women around me again I will leave you and you will never see me again. Rodney, Keyword If and when If we ever get married. I also ask that if we do grow apart that we remain friends." Rodney bends over again and kissed Karen on the lips and says " I love you so much and yes I can do that." "I don't know what I would do without you Karen. Karen smiles back at Rodney and lays her head back onto the pillow and closes her eyes. Mrs. Matthews walks into the room and almost drops the tray of food and realizes that Karen is so beautiful when she sleeps so she puts her head down and carries the food back to the nurse for the nurse to keep until Karen awakes again from her nap. Mr. Matthews grabs his wife and says lets go get some air and come back and I have already talked to Emma, Emma said that she would stay here until we get back. Mrs. Mathews looks at her husband and says " okay." Karen's parents walk away and Emma goes into Karen's room and sits down and notices the 10 karat platinum ring on Karen's hand. Emma covers her mouth and begins to pray and lay her head on Karen's bed. Rodney is sitting down outside Karen's room and begins to make a call to someone and then calls Karen's friends. Rodney is hoping that they will to come and see them both at the hospital. Rodney calls Brian and Keisha's house first and then decides he will call all the others shortly after. Rodney begins is looking up Brian and Keisha's number in his cell phone and a white woman comes over to Rodney and say's " are you NBA basketball star Rodney Rollins?" Rodney stands up out of his seat and says "yes, yes I am. " The woman says OMG my friends are not going to believe me. May I have your autograph and Rodney says yes and smiles and then the woman begins to grab something for Rodney to sign his autograph with. The woman asks if it is okay to also take a photo with her. Rodney smiles again and looks at her and says "sure, anything for my fans." The lady puts the paper away in her purse and grabs a phone out of her bag. The woman get really close to Rodney's face and put her face close to Rodney and strikes a pose for the photo. The woman takes two additional photos to make sure she comes out with a good photo. The woman thanks Rodney for his time and for taking a photo with her. The woman walks away and then gets on the phone and calls someone. Rodney sits back down and wipes the sweat from his forehead and tries to make the phone call to Brian and Keisha and again.

.

Chapter 2
The Truth Shall Set You Free

Keisha Alexander, Brian's wife is putting dinner together for her and Brian in the kitchen and the phone rings. Keisha walks over to the phone and says" hello." Brian replies back and says "how is my beautiful girl doing? Keisha replies back "I am doing well. I am making your favorite dinner tonight. Brian: I've got a surprise for you. Keisha replies back and says what is it...is it a ring? Brian answers back and says" No it is not, but do you want another ring? Keisha replies back and says "no honey my ring is fine. Brian then tells Keisha to guess again. Keisha says "okay hmm... is it a bracelet? Brian says "No, but guess again." Keisha tells Brian that she is not guessing again. Brian smiles to himself and says " I will be home shortly. Can I pick you up anything while I am out? I am really close to the house. Keisha says " hey so you are not going to tell me what it is? Brian tells Keisha no, but I will be home soon but thank you for asking honey. Keisha says "no but thank you for asking." Keisha tells Brian that she will remember this." Brian tells Keisha that he will be home soon and that he loves her. Keisha replies back and says" I love you too." Brian replies back and says" no Keisha Alexander I love you more." Keisha hangs up the phone and goes back to preparing hers and Brian's dinner. The phone rings again. Keisha looks at the phone and says I wonder who this can be now. Keisha stops what's she is doing and looks at the phone and then decided she is going to answer it. Keisha goes over to the phone again and puts down cooking towel. Keisha answers the phone and says hello. An unknown voice replies back and asks if Brian Alexander was at home. Keisha replies back and says" No, Brian is not here right now, can I take a message? Keisha goes to look for paper and pen to write. The unknown man says to Keisha please forgive me...you must be Brian's lovely wife Keisha. Keisha pats her hair and smiles as if she's looking into a mirror and says yes she is Mrs. Alexander. The unknown man says " I am Anthony Woods, Brian's friend from college. We used to attend Core House together and we were roommates. Keisha says "oh yeah! I have heard so much about you. It is great to finally meet you. Anthony replies back and says "could you tell Brian that I am in town for the week and I want to see him this week before I leave town. Keisha replies back and says "I sure will tell Brian the minute he gets in. Brian is also actual on his way home now. Anthony replies back and says" ok, it's a pleasure to talk with you Mrs. Alexander. My number is number is 555-555-1800 Keisha replies back and says '' ok I got it. Thanks for calling Anthony goodbye. Anthony replies back and says" good bye Mrs. before Anthony could finish saying Keisha's full name Keisha hangs up the Phone up on Anthony. Keisha places Anthony's number on the counter while putting down the phone. Keisha goes back and starts finishing up the dinner she was preparing. The phone rings again and looks up at the ceiling and says " God what are you trying to tell me?" Keisha walks over to the phone again and answers the phone and Rodney says "Keisha it's me Rodney, please don't hang up on me. I am at the hospital with Karen. Keisha says "Rodney is that you.....is everything okay? How is Karen? The doorbell rings.....Keisha pulls over her apron and tells Rodney to hold on and tells the person at the door that she will be right there. Rodney replies back and says "yes but make it quick. Keisha replies back and says " don't start you know I don't like you." and this better be a good reason why you're calling me. Rodney replies back and says" just hurry up and come back to the phone." Keisha lifts up her hands into the air and then puts them down while walking to the door. Keisha opens the front door and steps back and smiles. Keisha says " Hey girl" and Jasmine says " Hey girl" Keisha says' " hold on Jasmine I almost forgot I got someone on the phone come in and sit down and make yourself at home like you always do." Jasmine replies back and says " you know I know the routine and what do you have to eat. I am starving. Girl follow me to the kitchen so you can eat. Jasmine replies back and says: hey girl you look a little busy. If I need to come back another time I can. Keisha says" you are a little too late you should of thought of that before you came over without calling but you are my girl so you're okay. Jasmine smiles with a Big smile on her face. Keisha goes back into the kitchen and picks up the phone and says "are you still there? Rodney replies back and says "yes, and what took you so long? Keisha tells Rodney that she had to get the door and that it was a friend of hers and then tells Rodney hold'em up wait a minute...I am not your wife...why am I explaining myself to you?" Wait a minute, you just said you were at the hospital. Please get to the point and tell me what is wrong. Rodney says " I thought you'd never ask." Karen is in the hospital and I am here with her and I think it would do her some good if you come with Brian. The Dr. says she will have to be here for a couple of days because of the lump on her head. Keisha replies back and says " Oh My Gosh Rodney are you serious...what happened... how did she get that lump on her head." Rodney tells Keisha that he will explain everything once she gets to the hospital. Brian and I will be there as soon as he gets home. In the meanwhile stay by her side and don't let anything happen to her. Rodney replies back "oh believe me I will not let anything happen to my future wife." Keisha replies back wife.... Keisha replies back and says "Huh oh yeah you must of fell and bumped your head too. Rodney tells Keisha that he has to go the Dr. is waiting to talk with him. Keisha says " Okay hang in there and I will see you two soon. Keisha hangs up the phone and tells Jasmine that her best friend is in the hospital and that this is really is not a good time, but since she is already there she can stay. Jasmine tells Keisha that she is very sorry to hear the bad news but she has good news. Keisha tells Jasmine that she has 10 minutes to spills the beans because she has to finish cooking dinner for her and Brian. Keisha reminded Jasmine that Brian is on his way home. Jasmine says " I am glad you asked." Jasmine walks over to where Keisha is and stands in front of her and says " I am getting married Keisha." Jasmine points out her engaged finger and shows it off to her. The two women hug each other and sigh after being so excited. Keisha says girl I am so happy for you...we are getting married. Jasmine looks at Keisha and has this confused look on her face. Keisha looks at Jasmine and says " well you know what I meant. Keisha says "so have you picked out a date and do I know him? Jasmine pretends she does not hear what Keisha just said and says" can you be my wedding planner?" Keisha looks Jasmine right in eyes and says " Oh no I know you just did not ignore me." Jasmine goes on to say " well I have been dating this guy off and on for a while and he just suddenly asked me to marry him and I feel he could really be the one Keisha. Keisha says " well if you like him then I love him. Jasmine gives Keisha a dirty look and Keisha says to Jasmine " what I'm just saying....You like him I Love him. Whatever works for you and Mr. no show man of yours! Keisha tells" Jasmine I would love to be your wedding planner. Do you know what your colors will be? Jasmine replies back and says "yes I would love them to be....The front door opens and Brian comes in with his briefcase and lays it on the table and walks into the living room. Keisha tells Jasmine to wait there while she goes to greet her husband, because he might not be dressed all the way. Jasmine says " I forgot you and your husband was freaks. Keisha smiles and says " well it takes one to know one." Keisha wipes her hands on the towel and walks into the living room and tries to tell her husband that she has guest in the kitchen. Brian walks over to kiss Keisha and still starts dancing with her and Keisha laughs and says" it's not funny honey we really do have company in the kitchen." Brian says "oh really, ok let me put my shirt back on. I will be in there in a minute. Keisha wipes her forehead and walks back into the kitchen and says I am so happy for you Jasmine. Brian walks into the kitchen and tells Jasmine hello. Jasmine picks up her purse and says hello to Brian. Jasmine tells Keisha that she was just getting ready to go. Keisha tells Jasmine that she will walk her out. Jasmine is already out the kitchen door and walking towards the front door and waves good bye. Keisha turns around and Brian is right in front of her face and grabs her and says " now where were we?" Keisha hugs and kisses Brian and says " I am sorry baby but we have to wait to make love until we get home." Karen is in the hospital and they need to prepare to eat take out tonight because she does not know what time they will be home tonight. Brian hugs Keisha and says " baby I am so sorry" how did you find out? Keisha goes on to tell Brian that Rodney Karen's ex called her from the hospital. Brian then hugs Keisha again and tells her don't worry about finishing dinner we will eat takeout. Keisha kisses Brian and says I love you Mr. Alexander and I am ready to go when you are. Brian suddenly remembers the gifts in the car and ask Keisha if they could take her car. Keisha replies back and says "sure we can take my car." Brian says great I am going to go heat up the car now and I will come in and get you when the car is warmed up. Keisha says okay and goes into the bathroom and tries to apply some last minute touches of makeup on her face. Brian comes into the kitchen's back door and tells Keisha that the car is warmed up and it is time to go. Brian walks Keisha over to her side of the car and opens her door for and shuts the door and then walks over to his side of the car and gets into the car. Brian pushes the remote for the garage door to open and backs out and then makes sure the garage door comes all the way down and drives off to the hospital. Brian asks Keisha " how does she know where Karen is at? Keisha tells Brian that she and Karen are really close and that she knows just about everything about Karen. Brian says " okay if you say so, so where are going? Keisha says " I thought you would never ask." Brian says " oh you being a smarty pants huh...just wait till tonight. Keisha laughs and says "oh I' am looking forward to it." Keisha tells Brian to make a left at the light and to keep straight the private hospital will be on the right. Brian says " I did not know we had a hospital like this around our neck of the woods, wow this is a nice hospital. I wonder if they got an infant area." Keisha looks at Brian and then looks out the window. Keisha and Brian have been trying to have kids for many years but they have not been successful. Brian keeps his faith and believing that God is going to make a way out of no way. Brian parks the car and Keisha waits in the car while Brian walks over to open Keisha's door. Keisha gets out of the car and Brian shuts her door. Keisha grabs her blanket that was sitting in her lap and stands up and kisses Brian and says I am so in love with you and I can't wait to have your baby. Brian kisses Keisha and says "Keisha just keep believing and know that God will make a way." Keisha hugs her husband tightly as tears began to roll down her face. Brian feels the drops of tears on his shirt and tells her "hey beautiful I love you and know that God has the last word."

Our baby is on the way. Brian holds his wife while trying to hold back the tears and be strong for her and grabs her hand and begins to walk her into the hospital. Rodney is sitting down tapping the floor with his feet and jumps up as soon as he sees Keisha and Brian walk through the door. Keisha and Brian both hug Rodney and ask how he has been holding up. Rodney say's "I am okay guys, I am just worried about Karen. The Dr. says that because of the fall that Karen will have to be in the hospital for a couple of days." Keisha mouth drops open and looks like she is about to drop to the floor and Brian catches Keisha's fall and asks what caused Karen to fall? Brian tells Keisha to sit down and that he is going to order some food for them and ask Rodney what he wants to eat while he is ordering their food for the evening. Rodney replies back and says man I'll eat whatever y'all are eating. Rodney replies back saying "let me know when the food gets here and I will pay for it, it is the least I could do for you all coming to the hospital." Brian tells Rodney "he does not have to." Rodney then tells Brian, "man yes I do. I thank you guys are here. I called the others and they should be on the way here too." Brian asks Keisha "if she was okay?" Keisha replies back and says "she is okay and that she is just a little tired and with everything going on today it was just a little much. I am okay I am going to go see how Karen is." Brian walks over to Keisha and kisses her on her forehead and sits back down. Keisha walks into Karen's room and sees Karen's mother and father are sitting down in the room. Mr. and Mrs. Mathews stand up to greet Keisha and give her a hug. Mrs. Mathews tells Keisha" she is so happy to see her." The Mathews tell Keisha that they are going to step out and go get something to eat and that they will be back. Keisha nods her head and sits down right next to Karen's bed and Keisha begins to pray and lowers her head and suddenly Karen wakes up and see's Keisha right beside her grabs Keisha's hand. Keisha rises up her head and tells Karen that "she is happy to see her." Karen looks at Keisha and tells her she wants to go home. Keisha begins to cry and tells Karen " that she can't go home yet, but she will be able to go home soon." Keisha asks Karen "if she was hungry because Brian had just ordered some of her favorite food?" Karen smiled and tells Keisha "she is starved and that the hospital food is not too good." Keisha tells Karen that the food is already on the way. Keisha asks Karen does she think she can remember what could of caused her to fall. Karen had described what had happened this morning and then she began to talk about how Rodney showed up at her house and how she must had fallen from the conversation. Keisha tells Karen that she has to ask Karen a personal question. Keisha went on to say " did Rodney by any chance hit her." Karen started to laugh and smile. Keisha I am being serious Karen, Brian is right here and you know all I have to do is say the word and Rodney is gone." Karen begins to laugh again and says" no she wish he would, he would never play another game again." The women laugh together again and Brian comes into the room and announced that the food was here and offered food to the women. Brian makes Karen's plate and tells Karen it is so good to see her and that if she needs him or Keisha for anything that they just live not to far from the hospital. Rodney comes into the room and sits down and eats with everyone and then thanks Brian and Keisha for coming as the Rogers begin to come into the room and hug each other and offer if there were anything they could do for Rodney. Rodney stated no and they left and the Rogers come in and take a seat and by this time Karen has already fallen back to sleep again. Vicky and Kevin hold hands and pray for Karen and Rodney together and congratulated him on his engagement to Karen. The Alexander's arrive home and Brian grabs Keisha's right hand and he leads her to the sofa and tells her to sit down for a moment because he has to go outside to the car and get some things. Keisha I need you to close your eyes and don't peak and I will be right back. Keisha tells Brian okay. Keisha acts like she is really excited and she is has a big smile on her face. Keisha opens one eye while trying to keep one closed to see what he is doing and realizes she can't see anything so she gets up and heads to the front door and realizes that Brian is very close to the front door so she jumps up and runs back over to the couch and pretends she has had her eyes closed the entire time. Brian opens the front door and walks over to where Keisha is sitting at. Brian sits all the baby items on the floor. Brian says "ok Keisha open your eyes." Brian crosses his arms and smiles as Keisha opens her eyes and jumps back into the sofa and says Brian what is all of this...did you adopt a child? Keisha sighs and Brian grabs her hand. Brian asks "Keisha does she remember when he said that special prayer asking God to bless us with a child?" Keisha replies back and says "yes Brian I do remember, but I am not pregnant yet sweetheart, at least I don't think I am!" Brian asks Keisha does she believe in him when he tells her that they are about to be pregnant with their first child?" Brian tells Keisha that he had a dream the other night and that it felt so real. Keisha begins to say to "Brian baby...you okay?" Keisha starts touching on Brian's forehead and cheek to make sure he wasn't running a temperature. Keisha replies back and says "I just want to make sure that our child has everything he/she needs." Brian replies back and says" yes Keisha I am fine." I saw in a dream that we would be having a child soon." Keisha grabs Brian hands again and gives him a hug and kiss. Keisha tells Brian if you believe that God is going to bless us with a child, then I believe it too Brian, so where do we start? I am a great painter and speaking of painting. Where are going to paint at? All three rooms are full. Brian tells Keisha that he has decided to move everything out of his office and make his office the baby room. Keisha tells Brian that he is so amazing and good to her and what will she do without him in her life? The couples hug each other and stare into each other eyes. Oh Brian I almost forgot to tell you that you had a friend call you today by the name of Anthony Woods. Brian says "I have not seen this man in a long time. I can't wait to see him." Brian asks Keisha did Anthony say where he would be staying at this week? Keisha replies back and says "no but he did say that he would be in town for a week." Keisha also states that wrote his number down and it is on the kitchen counter for Brian to pick up. Brian gets up from the sofa and heads over towards the door and walks into the kitchen and makes the phone call to call Anthony Woods. Anthony answers the phone and Brian sits down and began to prepare himself because he knows that they will be on the phone for a long time. The men have not talked in a couple of years and there is so much to catch up on.

Chapter 3
Nothing Still Has Changed

Karen arrives home from the hospital and excited to unlock her front door. Rodney is following behind her carrying all the roses and cards from her family and friends. Karen unlocks and opens the door and puts her purse on the hall table and drops her mail on the sofa, while she walks around the house to make sure Emma has taken care of everything. Rodney comes out of the kitchen from putting up the cards and roses. Emma walks down the steps coming from cleaning Karen's up stairs part of the house. Emma and Karen hug each other and Emma heads to the kitchen to get Karen and Rodney something to drink. Karen flips on the radio and the first song that comes on is " I Wanna Dance with Somebody" by the late Whitney Houston. Karen begins to dance and bops her head to the beat while going through the mail and dishes out what is important and what's not at the moment. All of a sudden Karen stops and reads the letter that was sent to her from her lawyer. Karen put her right hand over her mouth says you won't get away with this Caroline Brinkley. Rodney comes into the room and finds Karen reading the letter and asks her if everything is all right. Karen yells out what are we going to do? How is this possible? The devil is a lie and the Brinkley's won't get away with this. Rodney asks Karen "what are you talking about?" and then the doorbell rings and Karen puts away the mail she just opened up and Rodney walks towards the door and unlocks it. Rodney yells you got guest beautiful. Karen comes to greet who's at the door. A man carrying two dozen of roses smiles at Karen and gives Karen the roses. Rodney tips the driver and shuts the front door and reaches over to kiss her. Karen looks at Rodney in the eyes and says "are you serious....Do you really want to marry me?" Rodney replies back and says "without a shadow of a doubt. I want to spend the rest of my life with you." Karen tells Rodney that she can't wait to spend the rest of her life with him. Although Karen still feels that there is something missing. Rodney put his arms around her again Karen hugs him back. Rodney takes the flowers from Karen and gives them to Emma to put into Karen's room. Rodney walks over to the couch and asks Karen what would she like to watch and while he prepares to cook for her. Karen is slow to respond. Rodney did you just say that you were cooking for me? Rodney replies back and says "yup you heard right." I will be cooking something for you tonight." Karen replies back " this I have got to see." while adjusting herself on the sofa to sit back and relax. Rodney slightly kisses Karen's hand while bringing Karen some wine to relax her. Karen tells Rodney that maybe they could go to a new French restaurant downtown? Rodney becomes a little edgy and walks away from Karen and walks back into the kitchen. Karen follows Rodney into the kitchen and asks Rodney what's wrong? Rodney replies back "we can go to any restaurant but that place." Karen replies back and says "Why not?" Rodney replies back and says" because I had a bad experience there and I rather not go there again." Karen replies back and says "wow, I can't believe you. So who did you go there with Rodney?" Rodney becomes very evasive and is slow to respond to Karen's question. Rodney replies back and "says I went with a few of my team mates." Karen replies back and says yeah right Rodney you took another woman to that restaurant didn't you?" Rodney tells Karen to please stop with all of the accusations. Karen tells Rodney that she can't see the change. Rodney replies back and says "Karen please don't say that." Rodney grabs Karen's hand but Karen pulls it away and then turns her back to him. Rodney replies back to Karen's body language and says "listen baby, I know I haven't always did right by you, but please don't give up on me." " In the past I had a chance to give you everything in my heart, but I blew it." I want to make it up to you." Karen is slow to respond but she begins to loosen up Karen tells Rodney" I know you're not perfect and neither am I, but I am a simple woman that don't require a lot to make me happen." All I need from you is those four letter words and your time I will be the happiest woman in the world." Rodney looks at Karen and smiles and says ah "four letter word.....hmm what could that be? Karen looks at Rodney and tells him " you play to much Rodney." Rodney then replies back and says "oh you mean the word Love." Rodney is slow to respond and grabs Karen again and tells her that he loves her. Rodney tells Karen that she knows that he loves her. Karen explains to Rodney that to love a woman is just not saying it and giving her a few gifts on special days and that he has to truly love her as a woman. Karen also went on to say that it has to come from his heart and soul. Karen also tells Rodney that a woman can tell you love her by the love for God that he has and by loving God and respecting God is an example of how he will love himself and her. Rodney replies back and tells Karen that he does love her from his soul. Rodney starts to take off his clothes and begins to try to undress Karen and Karen pulls back and says I' am sorry Rodney, but I am saving myself for you until we get married. Love making is really far from my mind right now and if we did make love then..... Well we would bring an innocent child into this world. Having kids out of wedlock is a sin. Rodney I believe that if you truly love me then you will wait for me. If you will be my husband and I will be would your wife, then we have nothing to lose! Rodney pulls Karen's close to him and picks her up and walks her up stairs and places her on her bed and asks her how they can make it happen right now between them and how can they get everything started first thing in the morning. Karen pulls away and says "no Rodney." Rodney begins to say to Karen "what, Karen I don't understand you. One moment you tell me that you can't make love to me until we marry each other and then I tell you let's go get married tomorrow it's still not enough for you." Karen please tell me the truth. Karen replies back and says "you see Rodney I said all of that and you still didn't hear me." I do hear you loud and clear Karen but understand that I have needs and wants too. Rodney tells Karen to please listen to him. The doorbell rings, Karen walks over to the bathroom and Rodney walks down the hall to greet whoever is at the door. Emma beats Rodney to the door and Rodney turns around and starts walking back to the living room. Emma lets Karen's friends in and tells them to sit down and make themselves at home and that Karen will be down shortly. Rodney walks past all the women while passing all the women on his way to the kitchen. The women reply and say hello. Karen walks down the steps and into the living room says "hey girls what are y'all up too?" Monica and Vicky walk up to greet Karen and they both hug Karen. Monica tells Karen that they came over to get in her business and that they saw a car in her driveway that didn't look familiar. Karen looks shocked at the girls and then tells the girls to please don't start this over protectiveness tonight. The women promised and agreed to not make a fuss over Karen's personal life. Monica detected an aroma of something nice being cooked in the oven. Monica looks at Karen and says whatever Karen, but Karen what is that smell in your kitchen. Karen replies back and says oh, that is something Rodney is cooking. Monica replies back "wait a min did you say Rodney is cooking for you tonight Karen." Karen replies back "yes Monica Rodney my man is cooking for me tonight." Monica replies back and says " wait a minute Karen did you just say your man?" Karen replies back and says "yes you heard right I said Rodney is my man." Monica replies back and says hmm well if you like it then I love it. Rodney walks out the kitchen and stands over by Karen. Rodney tells everyone Hello. Monica looks at Vicky and tells her I know he got something under his sleeve and she's going to find out whatever it is. Karen tells Monica to please be nice. Rodney replies back and tells Monica that It's ok and that sometimes people should watch what they are saying about people before it comes back to bite them. Vicky replies back to Rodney and tells him hello and that she will tell Kevin that he said hello. Vicky asks Rodney how is he doing and Rodney replies back and says" I am doing good Vicky". Vicky replies back Friday night. Vicky replies back to Rodney and says" Well I wish you and your team the best. Rodney replies back and says "Thank you Vicky." Vicky tells Rodney he is welcome. Monica then looks at Vicky and says "hey Vicky who's side are you on?" Vicky rolls her eyes at Monica and says don't go there with me Monica. Monica looks at Rodney and mouths to Rodney game ain't over yet. Rodney began to silently laugh in disbelief of Monica. Karen looks at Rodney to clear the air and for him to announce that they will be getting married. Rodney then nods his head back at Karen and then asks that everyone grab their wine glass to make a toast to celebrate Karen's and his engagement. Monica takes a sip then realizes that she needs to drink the whole glass and then blurts out and says Karen I can't believe this...Are you just going to stand there and let him do this? Karen I know you fell and bumped your head but come on you are not dumb or desperate. Karen replies back and says I am sorry Monica but the glass slipper fits and I am going to wear it. Monica's mouth drops wide open and then looks at Karen in disbelief. Monica replied back and said Karen I am sorry but I have to ask you does your Mother know about this. Karen begins to laugh and smile and tells Monica that she is a grown woman and that she does not need to have her or anyone baby sit her or make decisions for her. Karen tells Monica I am very sorry ladies but I think it's time that everyone leaves. Rodney looks really irritated at Monica as she walks past him. Vicky tells Karen and Rodney that she wishes them the best and that she will tell the others. Rodney walks over to lock the door and walks back over to Karen and kisses her forehead and walks over to get his hanging coat and scarf and tells Karen he thinks he should go too and that he will call her when he gets home. Karen agrees and follows him to the door and lets him out. Rodney reaches over one more time to kiss Karen and tells her that he will call her tomorrow and to get some rest. Karen replies back and tells Rodney good night Rodney I love you and Rodney tells Karen that he loves her too. Karen shuts the door and locks the door and leans up against the door and tells herself out loud "Why do I always attract the men who are dogs?" Karen sighs and then walks down the hall way and over to sit on the couch and plumps down. Karen closes her eyes and then remembers she hasn't eaten and then gets right back up and Emma comes into the kitchen and tells Karen to sit down and that she will get her food for her. Emma also asks Karen is there anything on her mind that she wants to talk about. Karen looks at Emma and smiles and says yes, but there is so much to talk about. Where does she begin to start? How does everything happen overnight? Emma walks over to Karen and hugs her and tells her to breathe my child trust and believe that everything will get better.

Karen smiles and says I hope so because if not I am in for the ride of my life. I have to admit Emma I believe Monica is right. I mean why does all of a sudden Rodney comes out of the blue and asks to me marry him? I Mean I do feel a little weird but at the same time it feels so right because I was in love with him and he has finally come back to marry me. This was my dream to marry him. Emma replies back and says to Karen I hate to admit it too Karen but I do see a change in Rodney and that Monica might be wrong, but I really think that time will tell. Just give it time and you will see don't make any hasty decisions. Rodney may have really changed his life for the better. Listen Karen you are my baby girl and I want the best for you but know that Rodney may or may not be your soul mate. Karen replies back and says yeah you're right Emma just give him the chance to show me and that time will tell, I pray that God will please show me the truth before it's too late. Emma serves Karen her food and tells her to eat up before her food gets cold. Karen never responds back and gives grace and begins to start eating her food. Karen's cell phone begins to go off and Emma tells Karen to sit and that she will get it. Emma comes back into the kitchen and tells Karen that's it's her mother on the phone and Karen tells Emma that she will take it. Karen answers the phone and says hello mother. Mrs. Mathews replies back and tells Karen that she hopes she is feeling better but she was not only calling to check on her but to warn her that they have an serious issue that has just occurred between them and the Brinkley's. Mother yes I know about what you are referring to, Mrs. Mathews replies back and says "oh you, do then what do you have in mind and have what in place? Well mother I plan to buy them out. The Brinkley's will not take over Ross's Oil and Gas that's for sure. They have no idea who they are dealing with since I have taken over. Mrs. Matthews replies back and says I think you are on the right track but I believe it's in your best interest, that you sit this one out Karen and let me and your father take over. Nonsense mom I can do it. I, I mean I can handle it. I will be at the board meeting bright and early set for tomorrow morning. Are you sure Karen because I want to make sure there are no problems and that everyone on the board knows what we plan to do tomorrow in the meeting? Karen replies back and says " yes mother, I can handle it mother." Mrs. Mathews replies back and says nonsense Karen I can hear it in your voice you are not ready but you better get ready....You don't know the Brinkley's like I know them. Not another word. Now be ready to greet me and your father and the rest of the board members in the morning. I will tell the rest of the family. Karen replies back and says yes mother. Please tell dad I said hello and that I will see him in the morning. Mrs. Matthews replies back and tells Karen that she will tell her father. Get some rest Karen and your father and I will see you in the morning. Karen hangs up the phone and continue to eat her dinner. Emma comes back into the kitchen and tells Karen to go and take a hot bath that she just ran for her to relax and enjoy her first night being home again. Karen nodded and finishes her dinner and takes a sip of her wine and walks up stairs with it in her hand and walks into her room and gets undressed and gets into the bubble bath that Emma made for her. Karen steps down into the sauna tub and lays her head back and closes her eyes and then her cell phone rings but she doesn't even tell Emma to bring her the phone. Emma comes on the speaker phone and asks if she wants to take the call from Rodney and Karen tells her to tell him she is preparing for bed and that she will call him in the Morning. Emma replies back and says good call Karen I believe you have had enough for tonight. Good night princess and if you need anything just ring my bell. Karen replies back and says " Thank you Emma...Good Night Emma." Karen lays her head back on her pillow cushion for her neck and closes her eyes and begin to cry because she is so mentally and emotional tired. Karen begins to ask the Lord to help her and to make every crooked line up with the word of the Lord. After Karen finishes praying she begins to wash off her body and rinses off and gets out of the tub and puts her favorite silk pajamas. Karen washes her face and then brushes her teeth and then looks at herself one last time before she gets into bed and smiles at herself and then heads into her warm satin sheets. Karen gets into the bed and pulls the covers up over her shoulders and closes her eyes and begins to fall into a deep sleep again and see's the unknown man again wearing all white. Karen is amazed again.

Chapter 4
The Unexpected

Mrs. Matthews is looking out the window and her husband Mr. Mathews is sitting down drinking coffee while waiting for all of the board members to march in one by one. Mrs. Mathews phone rings...without looking Mrs. Matthews turns the phone off and puts it back in her purse. The last person comes in and shuts the door. Mrs. Mathews greets everyone by telling them good morning. The board members reply back and say to Mr. and Mrs. Mathews "Good morning Mr. and Mrs. Matthews. Mrs. Mathews goes on to say to all the board members that she is glad that everyone could make it and that she is very sorry it has come to this, but she has to inform them that they have 48 hours or less to buy out Brinkley's Oil and Gas Company. We have to buy them out, before they buy us out. Does everyone understand what we are about to do? The board members look amazed and looked stunned and many mouths drop open at this point. Mrs. Mathew's states that she will be asking everyone to stay late today. Please make arrangements to be here for the whole day. Is everyone clear on what we are about to do? Mrs. Mathews requests that Rachael needs to have all the reports about Brinkley's Oil and Gas Company to her as soon as possible? Rachael replies back and says" I can have that for you in the next 2 1/2 hours, because I have to pull from all my resources. Veronica asks Miss Mathews are they financially able to purchase Brinkley's Oil and Gas Enterprises? Mr. Matthews replies back and says "yes Veronica, but it will take everything we got and then some to keep us a float after we purchase Brinkley's Oil and Gas Enterprises." Kennedy adds on to what Mr. Mathews was saying. With all due respect sir I too believe that you are making a great decision. I believe we should have brought them out a long time ago. Mr. Mathews I believe we will have more than enough.

Mrs. Matthews asks is everyone clear that Brinkley's Oil and Gas must be purchased before or within the next 48 hours, or we will lose everything me and my husband have worked for. Ross's secretary Essence walks in with a newspaper in her hand and a phone call note. Essence blurts out that she is sorry that she has to interrupt their meeting but Mr. & Mrs. Mathews I just wanted to inform you that Brinkley's Oil and Gas Company just went live talking about on every media platform there is and that the Brinkley's stated that they will be buying out Ross's Oil and Gas in the next 30 days. Oh! By the way Mrs. Matthews, Karen just called and stated she will be running late due to a tire problem, which she believes she can't fix on her own. Mr. Mathews gets up from his chair and starts walking around the table to greet his wife and reaches across the table to hug Mrs. Matthews to give her a hug and kisses Mrs. Mathews and walks towards the door as he is talking on his way out trying to get a hold of Karen but her cell phone is going straight to voicemail. Mr. Mathews looks at everyone in the room and tells everyone that they have too much to lose, keep me posted. Mr. Matthews announces to everyone that he is now leaving the meeting to help Karen. Mr. Mathews asks Essence to please locate Karen for him and give him the address to where she is located at and to tell her that he is on his way. Mrs. Mathews gets up from her chair and gathers her things and tries to make it out of the office before anyone can see her tears drop down her face. Mrs. Matthew's president tells every board member to grab sheets of paper, so that he can explain Mrs. Mathews plan of action to take over and sits back down at her seat and says "this is my plan to take over Brinkley's Oil and Gas Company. Veronica rises up and says…we got company that we don't want. Carolyn Brinkley pushes her way through the door into the office Essence rushes in behind her…I am sorry Mrs. Mathews but she just ran right past me. Mrs. Mathews gets up from her seat and tells Essence call the police, better yet close the door Essence, because Mrs. Brinkley is about to get the living day lights beating out of her for breaking and entering. Mrs. Mathews begins to take off her heels and her earrings.

Baldwin stands up and begins to be the ref between both women in the office. Have you two gone crazy Kennedy asks? Mrs. Brinkley tells Mrs. Yvonne Mathews... I am not scared of you, if anything I am scared for you because you won't have a house, car or business to sit in. Mrs. Brinkley tells everyone to take a good look at her face because she will be taking over the oil company. Mrs. Brinkley tells Mrs. Mathews if she were her to be sleeping with one eye open tonight. Mrs. Matthew's eyes get big because Karen and Mr. Mathews rush through the door. Karen tells everyone in a high pitched voice that she is sorry that she is late. How is everyone? Karen does not notice Mrs. Brinkley in the room. The security officer comes in and says "come with me Mrs. Brinkley, you are under arrest for breaking and entering. Mrs. Mathews asks Essence "who is the new body guard?" Essence replies back and says " the new security officer is named Michael Wallace." Mrs. Mathews: tell Michael he is fired once the police take Mrs. Brinkley away. Karen turns to her mother and approaches her to say "I am so sorry mother about what just happened here? Can you fill me in on what is going on? Mrs. Mathews replies back to Karen and tells her that she is fine and to sit down and have a seat. Karen sits down in the chair and looks down. Mrs. Mathews tells Rachel to please fill Karen in on everything. Rachel replies back to Mrs. Mathews saying "yes Mrs. Mathews. Karen we are going over the plan to take over Brinkley's Oil and Gas Company today...like right now we are taking over their company. Karen replies back to Rachel and says "well I have a plan as well to take over Brinkley's Oil and Gas Company. Let's review each other's plans and we can agree to disagree on which plan to use." Rachael looks over at Mrs. Mathews and Mrs. Mathews nod in an agreement and then looks at Karen and says very well then let's look at both plans and see what plan will work because we only have 24 hours to buy Brinkley's Oil and Gas Company out. The Staff continues to work and Karen realizes it's late and she had promised Keisha and the girls she would come by to see them. Karen tells everyone that she must go but if they have any questions to call her and she will answer. Rachael looks at Karen up and down and then shakes her head. Karen walks out of the room and pulls the ringing cell phone out of her pocket and answers the phone. Karen says hello and the voice of Rodney fills her ears and he tells her that he can't wait to see her again and if they see each other tonight. Karen tells Rodney that she wouldn't mind seeing him if she got out in time from being out with the girls at Keisha's house. Karen gets a beep from Keisha's text message telling her to not to forget their girls night out party tonight at her house. Karen gets onto the elevator and she is seeing a white man wearing all black and looks very unusual around their office, so she calls the security guard on duty and asks him to go walking around because of the man she saw and described the secretary stated that this man is not one of their staff members and he will get on it. The security guard asks Karen is she okay and if she needed him to walk her to her car and she replied back saying no, no thank you. Karen gets off the elevator and thinks she almost there to see another dark shadow however, she really can't see so she begins to walks fast to her car and gets her keys out of her purse and pushes the button on her car to unlock the car door. Karen gets to the car panicking and almost out of breath and sits down and looks in the back seats of her car and then locks the door. Karen says " it better be no one in my car or around my car or I know something. Karen puts her purse in the passenger seat and then thinks she sees another dark shadow in the rearview mirror in her car. Karen starts the car and backs out almost hitting the light poll in the parking lot and skirts off. Karen then puts on her seat belt and then tries to call the security guard officer but he does not answer. Karen then looks in the rearview mirror and a black car with black tinted windows pulls out of the same parking lot she was just in. Karen starts to get nervous and then grabs her phone and tries to call Keisha. Keisha does not pick up her cell phone. There is a four way stop sign coming up with lights and the light turned to yellow and Karen tries to slow down so she can see the person driving through her mirror in the car in back of her. The light then turns red and the car doesn't want to let Karen see who it is driving and the driver begins to go even slower and backs off and then light turns red and the unknown car switched lanes to make a left turn at the light as the lights then turns green for Karen to keep going. Karen still can't see so she gets upset and bangs on the wheel in her car with frustration. Karen's cell phone ring and Karen looks down at the phone and sees that it is Keisha returning her call back and Karen answers the phone and says "hello" Keisha replies back "Karen it's me you okay you sound weird right now is everything okay with you." Karen replies back and says "yes and that she will tell her everything when she gets there and to pour her a glass of red wine." Karen hangs up the phone and begins to look around for anymore dark cars like the one she had just seen, but there was no other car in sight. Karen deep breathes and closes her eyes and smiles and tells herself that she is going to be just fine. Karen finally arrives at Keisha's house and Karen pulls up in the driveway and gets out of the car and pushes the button twice on her alarm system for her car and walks up to the front door and peeps in and sees Keisha sitting down on the couch watching her favorite show. Karen then rings the doorbell twice and then Keisha looks up at the clock on her living room wall then gets up from the sofa and then yells out "who is it?" Karen is still waiting at the door and Keisha opens front door and says hello Karen and welcomes her in and gives her a hug. Karen smiles back and says hello Keisha. Keisha grabs Karen by the hands and tells her that she has so much that she wants to talk about, but first thing first let's get you your drink and come and sit by the fire place. Brian just made for them. The women step down and walk into the living room where the fire place is and Keisha sits down and grabs a bottle of red wine and Karen takes off her coat and sits down and Keisha grabs a wine glass and tells Karen to tell her when to stop pouring the red wine. Karen tells Keisha to stop, that's enough. Karen looks around and sits back on the sofa and closes her eyes and then Keisha tells Karen that her shoes are adorable and that she has to get some just like them. Karen tells Keisha well you can have them because if I almost got mugged tonight I would not been able to run in them. Keisha replies back and says! No what happened....What do you mean you almost got mugged. Keisha says' girl keep talking I think I need some popcorn listening to this story. Karen smiles and says, oh you jot jokes and says this is not funny Keisha. Keisha laughs and says you are right you are dead serious keep talking and tell me what happened. Karen begins to tell Keisha what happened and the doorbell rings again and Keisha's maid Erica says she'll get the door. Keisha and Karen look at each other and Vicky and Monica walk into the house and the women walk to meet each other half way and Erica the maid comes in and asks Keisha does she need anything and Keisha tells Erica to make some popcorn and to bring some extra wine glasses for the guest. Erica smiles and leaves the living room. All the women hug each other then sit down on the sofa and take off their coats. Keisha yells out you guys I want you to stop what you are doing and listen to what Karen had just experience at work tonight. Karen looks at Keisha with big eyes and then continued with the story and the doorbell rings again. Keisha's maid Erica comes out of the kitchen and drops off the wine glasses and the popcorn and walks over to the door. Erica answers the door and Jasmine walks in and greets everyone and Keisha gets up and says hello to Jasmine and introduces her to everyone. Everyone looks at Jasmine and waits for her to come into the living room and step down and stand up and give Jasmine a hug. Karen gets a weird feeling in her stomach and she doesn't quite move off the sofa just yet until Jasmine comes over to Karen and Karen still does not get up she just leans over to shake Jasmine's hand. Jasmine smiles at Karen and looks her up and down silently and then takes a seat next to Keisha on the sofa and grabs the glass of wine Keisha is trying to offer her, while taking off her jacket. Jasmine smiles again at everyone while she takes a sip of her wine and then turns her head and looks directly at Karen and then takes a sip, as to say underneath her breath that this toast is just for you. Keisha tells everyone that she is thankful that everyone could come out tonight and that she has gotten everyone something but they can open up their gifts later because she has to listen to Karen tell her what happened at the office building tonight. Keisha asks Karen to please finish talking and Karen nodded and began to talk about what happened. All the women were shocked and of course gave their 2 cents on what might have happened and what could happen if she don't get more lights around the building at night. Keisha is completely speechless and reaches over to give Karen a hug. The doorbell rings again this time Brian walks up and says to Keisha honey I got the door go ahead and sit back down it should be for me anyway. Keisha says okay and sits back down on the sofa. Brian walks to the door and opens the door and smiles really big when he sees his college friend Anthony woods on the other side of the door. Anthony says "hey man" and gives him their secret hand shake form their fraternity in college that they pledged together with at Coore House University. Karen all of a sudden gets this burst of happy nervousness in her stomach and she just starts smiling for no one reason. Keisha begins to look at Karen and looks at her secretly without words and tells her if she is okay. Karen looks back at Keisha and nods before anyone else can notice what the two of them have been smiling about. The two gentlemen give each other a hug then walk down the hallway and step down into the living room and Brian gets ready to introduce his wife Keisha to his friend Anthony Woods and all of a sudden Karen looks up at Anthony Woods and her mouth drops open and her right hand goes limp and spills the red wine all over the cream leather sofa and the glass drops and breaks on the mahogany wooden floors. Keisha rushes over to Karen and asks her if she is alright and helps her get up from the sofa and all the other women get up and try to get help with the spill from Keisha's maid Erica and the rest of the women help Keisha walk Karen into the kitchen and sit her down in the chair. Keisha rushes over to the sink and grabs a paper towel to wet and wrings it out and rushes over to Karen and wipes her face with the warm towel. Keisha starts yelling Karen talk to me are you okay…what's going on. You are scaring me. I have never seen you like this. Karen is still stunned at this time and she can't speak and she is trying to grasp for air but she can't and Keisha is telling Karen to try to calm down and try to take deep breaths to get oxygen flowing again. Keisha rubs Karen back and Karen begins to relax and calms down so she at least she can breathe correctly. All the other girls begin to start praying around Karen and then Karen lays her hand on Keisha stomach and says "Oh my gosh Keisha" that man in the other room was the man that I keep seeing in my visions that God keeps showing me. That man in the other room is my husband. Keisha gets so excited and says omg Karen this is the guy that you have been talking about? Karen nods her head and everyone comes over to hug Karen. Brian comes into the kitchen and asks if everything is okay with Karen. Keisha looks at Brian and says yelp everything is just fine and winks at Brian. Brian walks into the living room and then ask Anthony "what is the name of the woman who spilled the red wine all over the floor?" Brian smiles and says" she is a good girl her name is Karen Mathews." Anthony takes a deep breath and says hmm. Brian looks at Anthony and Anthony has this huge smile on his face and Anthony tells Brian that Karen is his wife. Brian tells Anthony now wait a minute skeeta you just met her. What are you talking about she is your wife. Man have you been drinking before you got here. Anthony tells Brian no man that's it I have not been drinking, that's just it I am sober and I have a sound mind and Brian walks over to Anthony and hold up two fingers and asks him to follow his fingers. Anthony pushes Brian's hands down and says man get away from me with that, I am trying to tell you the truth I have not been smoking nothing and I have not been drinking nothing that women in there is my wife. Brian looks at Anthony and tells him how do you know, how can you be so sure. Anthony tells Brian I don't know man but that is my wife. Anthony reminds Brian the time when he first saw Keisha and Brian told Anthony that Keisha was his wife and Brian looks at Anthony and says aw man I am so sorry man. It's like that man I am so happy for you, if you really believe that this is her man I am happy for you and I support you. The men give each other a hug and hive five and then they sit on the sofa began to clean up of what is left of the spill. Anthony tells Brian that man don't worry about the spill on the sofa that he will buy him a new sofa. Erica the maid comes down the steps with her cleaning supplies and bucket in her hands and looks at the men with a huge smile on her face and winks at Anthony and tells the men that she got it and the men sit down on the sofa and Brian asks Anthony what is he going to do and how is he going to tell her. Anthony tells Brian " I don't know right now but God does. I do know that I have a ball that I have tickets for that I want you and Keisha and Karen to attend. Brian smiles at Anthony and points at him and says "hey you the man" you got this and the men give each other high five and then Erica finishes cleaning up the mess and tells Mr. Alexander that she is going to go get more wine for everyone. Brian tells Erica that he appreciates that and then looks over at Anthony and Anthony has this happy humble smile on his face while he is praising the Lord for his goodness and mercy. Anthony began to shed tears during his praise and worship to the Lord and then Brian decided to get on his knees right beside Brian and began to praise the Lord too for his grace and mercy. Erica comes back with the wine quietly and then gently sits the wine and glasses on the coffee table and walks off and goes into the kitchen to check on Keisha and all the women. Erica looks at Karen and says you are a blessed woman and Erica walks to her living quarters of the Alexander's home. Keisha tells Karen to tell everyone about her dreams to catch everyone else up to speed. Karen looks at the women is slow to respond as she slightly smiles and takes a deep breath and exhales. Karen begins to speak out and says okay. The other night I had dream I met this handsome and Godly man and wait a minute, let me tell you he wasn't like any other man I have ever met before or seen. He was different. Monica butts in and says "did he have big feet...you know what that means?" The girls laugh and get serious again to listen to Karen talk. Vicky butts in and says Monica will you be quiet. Vanessa nods at Karen and tells her to go ahead and speak. Karen begins to speak again and says "well the dream I had was me and a man dressed in white dancing together and I could feel that he loved me a lot and that I loved him too...it was almost like we already knew each other. Monica blurts out again and says to "Karen I knew it, you'll about to get your freak on in this dream." Karen tells Monica" No it's not like that Monica." Keisha tells Monica be quiet so Karen can finish. Karen begins to tell the story again and says well after we danced it's like we became one and he began to feed me strawberries, we took walks in the park and all of sudden he told me to cover my eyes because he had a surprise for me. But when I awakened I began to cry and the Lord began to speak to me and tell me that I should get ready to marry this year. Karen said "from that day I been seen rings in commercials and on people's hands that stand out to me. Keisha says to "Karen OMG. Girl are you serious?" Vicky yells out wow Karen that is some dream. How do you feel about it? Karen replies back and says "well normally I don't get that excited about dreams but this dream really got my attention. Keisha tells Karen that she really does believe God is trying to tell you something Karen. Karen replies back and says "Like what?" Vicky butts in and tells Karen God is trying to tell you to stop wasting your time with Rodney and open up your heart to receive the man of your dreams. Keisha freely says to Karen that she has to agree with Vicky on this one. God is trying to tell you something. Karen is slow to respond. I have to be honest. I am confused because Rodney came over yesterday and he really wants to be back together. I believe God, but what's if it is only a dream nothing more... I should just stop dreaming and stop living in a fantasy world. Keisha tells Karen that it may only be a dream now, but God does make dreams come true so you got to keep the faith Okay? Vanessa tells Karen" yeah keep the faith Keisha... God can allow the man of your dreams show up in a blink of an eye. Karen's phone rings and Karen answers it and Karen says Hello. Rodney replies back and says "hey beautiful." Karen mouths with her lips to tell everyone that "It's Rodney" and points to the phone. Keisha and all the other girls start swinging and motion with their hands to the left... to the left while dancing with movements. Karen smiles really big almost about to laugh and says " I am out with the girls right now, can I call you back? Rodney replies back and says oh okay Karen I just...I just wanted to tell you how much I really miss you and I wanted to see how you are doing. I just wanted to see you tonight and see if you and I could talk like old times. I really do miss you and I don't want to make the wrong decisions anymore. Karen replies back and says "okay Rodney meet me at my house in an hour." Rodney tells Karen thank you for meeting with me tonight." Karen hangs up the phone and Jasmine is looking at Karen with piercing eyes while taking a drink of her wine and tells all the women that she has to go and thanked Keisha for inviting her over. Jasmine walks out the kitchen door and all the women walk out of the kitchen and tell Jasmine goodbye and Keisha tells Jasmine that she will walk her outside and Jasmine replies back and says "thank you, but little shadows don't scare me." Karen looks at Keisha and then Keisha tells Jasmine goodbye and to call her when she gets home. The girls all gather around each other on the sofa and each of them grab a wine glass and wait their turn to pour fresh red wine into their glasses. Brian and Anthony step back into the room and Karen gets nervous again and Keisha looks at Karen and motions for her to breathe and Karen began to smile and take deep breaths and then Brian looks at Karen and then looks at Keisha and comes behind Keisha and gives her a hug and wraps his hands around her. Anthony finds a chair to sit in and tells everyone hello and Brian begins to take over the conversation and tells everyone that this is his friend from college and that he is happy Anthony is here. Anthony takes a look at Karen and winks at Karen. Karen tries to smile back without smiling too big. Keisha and Brian's eyes get big as they oversee the love and physical attraction in the room. There is a knock at the door and Brian gets up to get the door and Eric and Kevin say hello and the two men walk in together into the house and say to Brian" What's going on man? Anthony gets up from his chair and goes to go meet the other men in the hallway and Eric and Kevin see Anthony and say " man where have you been?" " We haven't seen you in a long time. How you living and where you Living? It's like Jesus, Jesus awe, awe every time I talk and walk he comes over me. It's like Jesus, Jesus. The women laugh and hug and greet their husbands as they come into the living room. Anthony smiles and looks at Karen and asks to sit down next to her. Brian begins to try to get everyone quiet and ask all the men "how did they know that the woman in their life was going to be their wife? Brian hugs Keisha and says he wants to go first. Brian begins to speak and says that he knew that Keisha was the one is when they would talk to each other they never wanted to get off the phone with each other and that they had so much in common and had the same faith values. Everyone looks at Brian and Keisha and says awe this so beautiful. Brian grabs Keisha's hand and kisses it and rubs her tummy. Karen looks at Keisha and then Keisha smiles back with a natural innocent look. Karen mouths to Keisha and says to "let me find out." Karen and Keisha blush and smile. Anthony looks at Karen and then looks away as soon as she looks his direction. Kevin blurts out and says I want me and my baby to next and tell everyone how I knew that Vicky was my wife. Kevin began to say " I knew Vicky was going to be my wife when I asked God to allow me to see her, so that I would know her before I met her in the flesh. The Lord answered my prayer and he gave me a vision of my wife a year later. I met my wife at the court house. Anthony blurts out saying " wow everyone has such an amazing story. I can only say that I've..... Karen's phone starts to ring and she is puts her wine glass down and searches for her phone and finds it and see's that it is Rodney. Karen answers the phone and says hi I am on my way, I was just leaving. Keisha looks at Karen and then Karen stands up and hangs up the phone and tells everyone good bye. Anthony stands up and offers to help Karen put on her jacket. Karen accepts and Karen tells everyone good bye. Anthony asks if he can walk Karen to her car. Karen replies back and says yes. Anthony looks over at Brian and winks his eye. Karen blows a kiss to everyone and walks out the door and Karen searches for her keys to push her alarm button and unlocks her car. Anthony opens up Karen car door and Karen looks around in the car first and then sits down into the car and starts the engine. Anthony asks Karen what is her name and Karen replies back and says Karen, Karen Mathews. Anthony is blown away by the news he just heard and Anthony replies back and says " the Karen Mathews over Ross's Oil and Gas Company?" Yes, I'm the Karen Mathews of Ross's Oil and Gas Company. Why do you ask or look so shocked? Anthony starts to reply but is hesitant and says well I know you have to go and I hate to keep you but perhaps we can talk about this over lunch or dinner some time. Karen replies back and says that's a deal and Anthony reaches in his pocket to give Karen a ticket to the ball and get one of his business cards out of his wallet. Anthony hands over the ball ticket and his business ticket and smiles and tells Karen that he hopes that he sees her again and that she have a good night. Anthony grabs for Karen's hands and kisses it and Karen smiles back at Anthony and tells him thank you and that she will be calling him. Karen takes her hand back and rolls up her window and drives off. Anthony stands back from the car and looks up at the sky and points and smile and says " Thank you for sending me my wife." A tear starts to come down Anthony's face and Brian looks out through the glass screen door and does not see Anthony anywhere. Brian then opens the screen door and walks outside to see if he sees his friend. Brian looks over to his right and see's Anthony is on his knees bowing down to God. Brian walks over and begin to pray in silence for Anthony. Anthony starts trying to get up and Brian stretches his hand out to Anthony and say's you have everything you need now Mr. Billionaire! Anthony looks up at him and smiles and reaches out to grabs Brian's hand and Brian lifts him up and they hug each other and pat each other on the back and say together "we are blessed to serve and awesome God and to be married to beautiful and talented women in our life's. The two men hit high fives and Keisha walks out with the guest. Brian and Keisha's guest began to say good night to Brian and Anthony. The guests get into their cars and drive off. Anthony grabs the tickets out of his suit coat pocket and gives the tickets to Brian and tells Keisha it was an honor to meet her and then Anthony gets into his car and then drives off. Brian grabs Keisha hand and kisses it and walks with her into their house. Brian shuts and locks the door behind them and then lays on it and smiles and pulls Keisha close to him and say to Keisha "Thank you for making me one of the most luckiest men on earth." Keisha looks at Brian and draws near to his face and tilts her head and closes her eyes and kisses Brian on the lips. Brian stops kissing Keisha and picks up Keisha and walks her up stairs to their bed room. Keisha says to Brian " I just got one question to ask you." Brian replies back and says you better hurry up and ask because there is not going to be any talking once we get into our bedroom. Keisha laughs and says okay. Brian did I just over hear you say that Anthony was a billionaire? Brian laughs and says " I knew you had special go-go gadget eye sight but I didn't know you had special hearing capabilities too. Keisha laughs at Brian looks Brian up and down and says and don't you forget it. I got it all and snaps her fingers and says just answer the question why don't you. Brian laughs and says yes Anthony Woods is a billionaire but you don't go off and tell Karen or anyone else. I know how you women are. Brian and Keisha arrive in their bedroom and Keisha jumps out of Brian's arms and points her two middle fingers into Brian's chest and says wait a minute hold 'em up what do you mean by you know how us women are? Brian starts to try to clear up that he was not talking about her but other women in general. Keisha explained that her and her friends were millionaires and the needed to clarify some more on who he was referring to. Keisha I meant to say women that I've dated in the past were gold diggers and that he did at one time date a couple of women who just wanted him for his money. Keisha replies back and says okay I am just making sure because you know with or with you I am a millionaire. Brian smiles and looks at Keisha and says I know honey how could you ever let me forget that you can carry your own weight around here and make more money than me in the past. Keisha replies back and says "awe honey I did not mean it like that but you know I had to set you straight. I married you knowing that you could not do anything for me but love me. Brian looks at Keisha and tells her I am glad we agree because quiet as keep that's why I married you too. Brian goes on to say I married you Keisha because I knew you could not cook, clean and never the less knew anything about how to pay bills, but I married your little crazy self anyway because I loved you and that didn't matter to me. Keisha's mouth has completely dropped wide open at this time. Keisha looks around to see if she can find a pillow and she finds the closest pillow next to her and swings it at Brian's head and Brian picks up another pillow and swings it at Keisha and hits her on the side. The two of them fall back onto their bed pillows on the bed and starts to kiss each other. Keisha stops kissing Brian for a moment while he is still kissing her on her neck and Keisha goes on to say baby did you really mean that about my cooking skills. Brian smiles and replies back and says "oh I meant every word but I still love you and you are getting better at cooking." Keisha raises her left eyebrow and squints her eyes and looks Brian dead in the eyes. Brian stops and starts to kiss and bite Keisha face and Keisha begins to laugh and they both start laughing at each other and Brian grabs Keisha close to him and lays her head on his chest and rubs her back and falls asleep. Keisha stares up at Brian and watches him sleep and then falls asleep shortly.

Chapter 5
The Golden Rule

Karen looks around her house one last time as she unlocks her car with the remote and steps into her car and starts up her engine and looks in the rear view mirror and sees no one there she puts her car in reverse and backs out of her garage and drives off. Karen notices an unfamiliar car parked almost like the one she seen the night before, but could not really tell so she doesn't think anything of it until she gets down the road a little bit and the car pulls out of its parking space and drives slow on purpose and flashes it lights at Karen. Karen really does not pay attention to what the car is doing because she is trying to search for a good channel on the radio. Karen finally gets to a channel she likes and the song comes on " Yeah I wanna dance with somebody….I wanna feel the heat with somebody, with somebody who loves me" by the late Whitney Houston. Karen smiles and lets the roof top down on her car and smiles and then all of a sudden she notices the same car that she saw the night before and tries to not look so obvious and looks for her phone to tell her mother and father that she is on her way to the office and that she will be seeing them shortly and that she loves them. Mrs. Mathews replies back and says Karen I love you too but be careful. Karen goes on to say that she will see her and her father soon. Karen tries to act like she is enjoying the nice crisp morning and pretends that she is looking for something and pulls over to an abandon gas station trying to let that dark black tinted car pass her. Karen is trying to see if she can get a good close up look at the driver. Karen turns down the music and notices that her phone is ringing and it's Monica. Karen answers the phone and says hey beautiful. Karen is still looking for the car because the car should of passed her by now, so she is getting a little confused. Monica replies back and says "Hey butterfly how is it going? Karen replies back and says everything is going good. Monica goes on to say that she is sorry about the way she acted the other night. Karen says you are forgiven and smiles to herself and Monica says " Okay now that we got that off our chest what's up with that Ooh wee I can barely contain myself Karen laughs and tells Monica to go on with what she was talking about. Monica goes on to say that BMW! Karen laughs and says Monica what are you talking about I don't have a BMW and you know that. Monica laughs and says no girl I know you don't have a BMW car but you do have a black man working. The two women laugh and Karen begins to hear a car engine. Karen hears a car around her but does not know where it is coming from. Monica is going on and on about Anthony Woods, the fine tall light skinned man at Keisha's house. Karen laughs again and says "' a black man working wow Monica what am I going to do with you." Karen tells Monica that she literally has to go and gets off the phone and that they will talk later this evening and hangs up the phone and puts the car in drive and pulls off back onto the road and looks in her rear view mirror. Karen does not see a thing so she gets back on the phone and calls her dad and tells him what just happened and her dad tells her to not to stop again and to hurry up and get to the office. Karen tells her father okay and she hangs up the phone and drives straight to the office and pulls up into the private drive entry garage to her office building and her father notices her pulling up and meets Karen at the elevator. Karen gives her father a hug and kiss on the cheek and says hello. Mr. Mathews asks Karen if she is okay because she sounded worried on the phone earlier. Karen replies back and says yes dad I am worried someone keeps following me in a weird all black tinted windows car. Mr. Mathews crosses his arms and puts his right hand up to chic and looks very puzzle hmm Karen I don't know of who it could be but lets go upstairs and see who it could be. Mr. Mathews pushes the floor that they need to meet the rest of the board members. The elevator doors open and Mr. Mathews says to Karen after you my dear and Karen walks into the elevator and then Mr. Mathews looks to the left and to his right because he thought he saw a dark shadow and tries to stall as he takes another brief moment to get onto the elevator. Karen looks at her father says dad are you alright? Do you see anything dad? Mr. Mathews says yes, yes of course sweetheart I am fine. I just thought I almost saw something too but I guess I didn't. The elevators doors shut and Baldwin comes around the corner and has the phone up to his ear and says to the man on the phone that he needs to have good news or else. The man replies back and says you need to meet me in person and you better have my money in full. Baldwin stops in front of the elevator and tells the man on the phone " you better do what you have to do or Mrs. Brinkley will have us both killed and I am not dying for you. If I have to get rid of you, I won't think twice Carson about doing it. The elevator doors opens and Baldwin hangs up the phone and steps into the elevator. Baldwin's phone rings again and Baldwin picks up the phone again and says hello. Mrs. Brinkley replies back and says " It's going to be your worst enemy if you don't have Karen killed in the next 24 hours." You got me Baldwin or it's going to be you killed. Baldwin swallows hard and takes a deep breath and replies back and says I am already on it and it will be done you have my word. Mrs. Brinkley replies back and says " this is music to my ears, now make it happen." Mrs. Brinkley hangs up on Baldwin and the elevator doors open to the 8th floor to meet with the Mathews. Baldwin hangs up his phone and puts it into his jacket and walks off the elevator and into the double glass doors to meet with the Mathews. Baldwin swallows hard again and opens the door and puts a quick smile on his face and greets everyone in the room. Karen notices something wrong but she can't put her finger on it. Baldwin picks a chair to sit in and Mr. Mathews greets Baldwin back and Mr. Mathews begins to finish talking about their plan to take over the Brinkley's Oil and Gas Company. Baldwin sits back into his chair and smiles at Mr. and Mrs. Mathews and rocks back and forth. Baldwin gets a text on his cell phone and Baldwin pulls out his phone and reads it and it's a message from Carson saying that the car is now ready for Karen to get into. Baldwin looks up at everyone and looks around and Mr. Mathews is still talking about the plan to buy out the Brinkley's Oil and Gas Company. Baldwin texts back well now you know where to meet me at and be there at 7p.m. and don't be late. Baldwin looks up and smiles at Karen and then over to her mother Mrs. Mathews.

Karen is trying to stay focus but she can't help but to glance over at Baldwin every now and then to see what Baldwin is up to during the time her father is talking in the meeting, because he has been missing lately since the Brinkley's announced that they were trying to buy and take over. Mrs. Mathews looks up at Karen and asks Karen does she understand the plan. Karen replies back and says yes. Baldwin stands up from the table and says with all due respect Mr. and Mrs. Mathews I fully understand your plan but I am sorry I must go. My family will be celebrating tonight for some things to finally take place in our lives and I must go. Mr. and Mrs. Mathews stand up and agree to let Baldwin go early to go and celebrate with his family. Baldwin walks over to Karen and tells Karen to have a safe trip home and it was great to see her again. Karen looks at Baldwin and then looks at her mother and then shrugs away from Baldwin. Mr. Mathews looks over at Karen and Mr. Baldwin and looks puzzled. Baldwin walks out the door and tells everyone good night and if you all need me please don't hesitate to call me for any reason. Mr. and Mrs. Mathews look at each other and then Mrs. Mathews steps out the room and waits till she see Baldwin get on to the elevator and makes a phone call in to Ronald which is her families hit man. Ronald picks up and says hello. Mrs. Mathews replies back and says " Ronald it's me Mrs. Mathews listen you got a minute" and Ronald replies back and says " you know I always have time for you what is going on? I believe that Baldwin is up to something but I can't put my finger on it can you have him followed please? Mrs. Mathews the pleasure is mine. It is already done. I will talk to you in a couple of days and give you my report. Mrs. Mathews replies back very well then plan to meet me by the lake and I will have your money for you when I arrive. Mrs. Mathew's smiles and hangs up the phone and walks back into the office and comes over to hug Karen and then her husband and tell them she loves them and that their family is going to win this battle. Mrs. Mathews kisses Karen's forehead and tells her to go home and get some rest and that she will see her in the morning for their daughter and mother brunch they have every week. Karen smiles and puts on her coat and prepares to walk out of the office and looks back and tells her mom and dad that she loves them and then turns around and a tear begins to run down her face as she gets onto the elevator. Karen steps off and she pushes the alarm on her car and Rodney pops out from the side of her car and says " boo" Karen almost loses her breath and Rodney comes up and grabs Karen from almost falling over. Karen catches her breath and takes a swing at Rodney. Rodney why would you do that? That was so mean. Rodney replies back and says "awe Karen I am so sorry I really didn't mean to scary you that bad. Karen are you okay?" Karen replies back yes. Rodney says " let's go to your house and then we'll jump in my car and then we can go on a dinner date." Karen smiles and says okay. Rodney pulls a dozen of roses from out underneath his back and gives them to Karen. Karen smiles and walks over to Rodney and says thank you and then opens her car door and looks around to see if she sees anyone. Karen doesn't see anyone so she gets into the car and puts the dozen roses' in the seat floor of the car. Karen reaches for her car seat and puts it on while looking in the rearview mirror. Karen puts the car in reverse and backs out and comes out of the garage and drives slowly to the entrance of Ross's Oil and Gas entrance and waits for Rodney to come around the corner. Karen begins to look around and starts to get nervous because she believes that Rodney should already have came around the corner she honks her horn and then Rodney drives around the corner slowly and motions to her to go on. Karen then grabs for her sunglasses in her purse in the passenger seat and puts them on. Karen turns on her right blinker to signal to Rodney that she will be making a right turn out of the parking lot. Karen pulls out of the parking lot and immediately turns on her left blinker to signal she will be making a U-turn in the left lane when the light turns green. Karen looks back at Rodney in the rearview mirror and Rodney is blowing Karen kisses from his car. The light turns green and Karen makes the U-turn and she can't see Rodney in her rearview mirror anymore so Karen begins to look to her left and then to her right and then she sees Rodney trying to tell her to race him to her house. Karen pushes down her automatic window button on her car to roll her right passenger window down to talk to Rodney. Rodney motions for Karen to get ready to burn by his skills of drag racing. Karen removes her sunglasses from her face and says really loud to Rodney "don't let this pretty face fool you. I can drag race too boo." Karen smiles at Rodney and then lowers his shades and Rodney looks back at Karen and looks up and down and says please "Miss I'm going to lose this race." Karen squints her eyes and raises her eyebrow and then prepares to take off. Karen utters underneath her breath and says " no you are not smoky and smiles with a smirk on her face. Rodney yells out and tells Karen that whoever wins between the both of them has to pay for dinner for tonight for whomever makes it to her house first. Rodney looks at Karen and then rolls up his windows and prepares to take off. Karen pulls off and begins to pick up speed and Rodney is trying to keep up and really is impressed how Karen is going in and out of lanes. Rodney yells out in dead silence of his car and says' "Let me find out that you do this for a living" Miss I don't do nothing wrong. Rodney begins to lose speed and he tries to make a combat by trying to stay hugged to the left side of the curb to give him more speed. Rodney begins to panic because he believes that he might actually lose in their bet. Karen gets ready to switch another lane a quarter mile from her house all of a sudden her car spins out of control and then hits a telephone pole and then turns over on its side and then catches on fire. Karen's body gets thrown into the window with only one side of her face showing along with the yellow roses that Rodney had just given her. Rodney drives up and begins to shout and says " no" while getting out of his car and runs over to Karen's car. Rodney tries to think really fast because he knows he doesn't have long to get Karen out of the car before it blows up in flames. Rodney begins to panic and walks back and forth and for a moment and then goes to his car and opens the car door and pushes the button to unlock his trunk and then walks over to his trunk and grabs his crow bar out and runs over to Karen's car and begins to bang on the window and the glass window shatters and then Rodney grabs Karen out of the car and goes back into the car and grabs Karen's purse. Just moments right after Rodney picks up Karen form the car, the car makes a loud noise and burst into flames. Rodney falls to the ground with Karen still in his hands. Rodney begins to scream and cry out to the Lord "God please help me and don't let my baby cry." Rodney's tears begin to drop on

Karen's face and Rodney begins to wipe off her face and tries to clean off Karen's dirty face. Rodney begins to search for his cell phone and remembers that his cell phone is in his car. Rodney looks up into the sky and asks God to forgive him for getting ready to look inside Karen's purse to get her cell phone out. Rodney locates Karen's cell phone and dials 911 and begins to talk to the 911 operator. Rodney begins to see a black car drive up slowly but can't make out who it is, so he begins to get up while still talking on the phone to the police and tries to flag the unknown car down. The car begins to drive faster towards him and Karen and then he tells the police that they need to hurry up and hangs up the phone and comes to pick up Karen and moves her to another safer side for them both and then looks around for the black car with tinted windows outlined in silver. Rodney begins to look to his left and then to his right to try to see who it could have been who wanted to try to hurt him and Karen. Rodney is very nervous and mad at this time and he starts digging for the cell phone again to call his body guard JT money maker. Rodney dials JT's number and JT answers and Rodney blurts out and says "man I really do need you right now, like in right now. JT replies back and "says alright man whatever you need I got you." Rodney tells him where to meet him at and tells him he better come packing." Rodney is unaware of what might happen. Rodney hangs up the phone and begins to dial Karen's mother and father's phone number. Rodney waits for either one of them to pick up but no one answers. Rodney leaves a message about Karen being in a bad car accident and that they need to go to Charles Adams private hospital and hangs up the phone. Rodney begins to see flashing red and blue lights driving up from the police and firefighter trucks. Rodney gets up the ground and tries to wave with both hands the police men down to where he and Karen both are. Two police cars pull up along with a fire truck and then shortly thereafter the ambulance pulls up and the paramedics jump out and run over to Karen and Rodney. The police get's out of the car and walks over to Rodney and says " is everyone alright?" Rodney replies back and says " yes, I am alright but I don't know if she is okay" please have someone check her out." The policeman yells out to Rodney that they will take good care of her. Rodney begins to see the black car with tinted windows again outlined with silver and he runs over and tries to tell the police that there was a car that was trying to run him and Karen over and the police man turns around to where Rodney is pointing to and then the car pulls off really fast and then the policeman begins to run towards the car while grabbing his gun out of his gun holder and tries to run up on the car and then stops to aim and get a good shot at the car. The second policeman there gets into his car and tries to follow the car that his partner was trying to shoot at. The first policeman makes a call in for back up and then describes the car and the roundabout location about where they are. The policeman walks over to Rodney and tells him it's not safe and that him and Karen have to go. The policeman tells the ambulance to wrap everything up and to finish everything inside the truck. Rodney walks over to Karen and gives her a kiss on her forehead and then rubs her cheek. The cell phone in Rodney's pocket begins to ring and go off then Rodney answers the phone and Rodney says hello and JT replies back and says hey man where are you at I don't see you. Rodney begins to explain to JT where he is and then the policeman yells at Rodney to wrap it up that they have to go. Rodney then tells JT don't worry about coming to where he first told him to just meet him at Charles Adam's private hospital off of Greenwood Street. JT replies back and says "you got it man, I am on my way. See you there in a minute. Rodney pushes end on the cell phone and runs over to where him and Karen was sitting at before the police came and grabs Karen's purse. Rodney swings Karen's purse over his shoulders and begins to run over to his car. Rodney opens up his car door and gets in and starts the engine and puts his car in drive and puts his seat belt on and pulls off to follow the ambulance and the policeman. Karen's cell phone goes off again while Rodney is driving and Rodney reaches for the cell phone and slides the screen over to answer the phone call and Rodney replies back and says hello and Mrs. Mathews replies back and says Rodney is that you? Rodney replies back and says yes Mrs. Mathews it's me Rodney, hey listen Karen has been in a terrible car accident we are now on our way to the Charles Adams private hospital. Mrs. Mathews does not respond because she has fainted so Mr. Mathews grabs the phone and yells out " hello, hello Rodney is that you? Yes, Mr. Mathews I was just trying to tell your wife to meet me and Karen at the Charles Adams private hospital and that Karen was in a bad car accident but she is now stable by the paramedics in the ambulance. Mr. Mathews replies back and says okay Rodney we are on our way. Rodney pushes end on the cell phone and puts the cell phone on his lap and begins to look around for the car that tried to run him and Karen over. Rodney blurts out and says to himself " something is really wrong, I've never known Karen to have any enemies. Whatever it is I am going to figure it out. Karen's cell phone rings again and this time Rodney waits for the person to say something because he looked at the number and the number doesn't look like any of the numbers he has been dialing. JT yells out hey man you there, Rodney answers back and says " oh yeah man it's me I am here. JT replies back and says this is my other cell phone and I am already here waiting inside for you. Rodney tells JT thank you and we are pulling into the hospital emergency entrance right now. Rodney gets out of his car and tells the valet parker to take good care of his car and to keep his change and to bring his keys to him when he finishes and that they will be on the 8th floor. Rodney goes through the emergency entrance and sees JT on his left side of the entrance and walks over to JT and JT and Rodney do their secret hand shake and then give each other hugs. JT yells out man you okay, Rodney replies back and says no man a man in an unknown car tried to run me and Karen over. JT replies back and says awe man you just say the words and I will take care of it. Rodney replies back and says man that's just it, I don't know who it could be. JT looks at Rodney with a confused face and then covers his mouth with his hand and says "oh my gosh, man you are serious." Rodney replies back and says man this is real I don't know who it is or who it could be, but the thought that comes to my mind from the looks of the car it's the Mafia. JT replies back and says " for real man, Rodney replies back and says this is so real right now and I got to get to the bottom of this. JT tells Rodney to go and stand with Karen now and check on her. Rodney leaves JT's side and finds Karen and then a heavy set Caucasian woman, who looks to be Karen's nurse says I am sorry but who are you? I have special instructions to not let anyone back there from Mr. Mathews Karen's father. The police comes up and tells the nurse that Rodney is Karen's fiancé and the nurse says okay and lets him through. Rodney looks over at the policeman and tells him thank you and that Karen's parents should be here any moment now. The policeman nodded and Rodney opens the door to Karen's room. Karen is a sleep and has lots of machines tied to her. Rodney comes and stands over her trying not to be loud and bends over to kiss her lips and grabs her hand. Karen grabs Rodney's hand back and smiles in her sleep. Rodney sits down feeling hopeless and worried about everything that had just happened. The Mathews burst through the door and Rodney wipes his eyes and reaches over to hug each of the Mathews. Mr. Mathews takes a look at Karen and walks over to the left side of Karen's bed and whispers in Karen's ear and says "hang in there princess, your daddy is here now." Karen still can't open her eyes but a single tear rolls down her face on her right side of her face. Mr. Mathews is touched and moved by this and grabs Karen and holds her and buries his head in her chest. Rodney notices it too and he has to step out of the room because he can't take seeing Karen like that. Rodney walks out of the room and tries to find the closest bathroom and finally sees one and walks into the bathroom. There is only him and a man that looks like he is from Italy, but Rodney can't tell what the man is. Rodney goes over to the stall that is directly in back of his across the divided bathroom stalls and as Rodney begins to undress and use the bathroom the man starts to zip up his pants and walks over to wash his hands and Rodney begins to try to focus on what JT and him were just talking about when he arrived to the hospital. He begins to dry off his hands and throws his paper towels in the trash and reaches for something in his pocket and grabs out a signature monogrammed handkerchief that read the letters CRM in gold thread. The man walks by Rodney and covers his mouth and says "Maybe there won't be a next time." Rodney looks back and to the side of him and the man dashes out of the bathroom. Rodney starts trying to finish using the bathroom and zips up his pants and then dashes out the bathroom but the man wearing all black had vanished. Rodney looks again to his left and to the right and then straight ahead again and still could not see anything. Rodney turns back around and heads back into the bathroom and washes his hands and fixes his clothes and looks himself in the mirror and puts balls up his head and hits the glass mirror. Rodney tries to get a hold of his self and heads out of the bathroom walks down the hall while still looking for the man he had just seen in the bathroom. Still no trace of the man he just seen in the bathroom. Rodney walks over to JT and tells him what just happened and JT stands up and says man I got this I am getting ready to call my boys and you stay here close to Karen and don't let her out of your sight. In the meantime I need you to describe the man to me so I can be on look out for him too. Rodney began to describe the man to the best of his knowledge and JT tells him okay again go and stand by Karen's door and make sure that you don't let anything happen to her Rodney. Rodney nodded and then walks away and heads to Karen's room. Rodney opens the door to Karen's room and notices that she is up and she has a big smile on her face. Rodney walks over to her and gives her a hug and a kiss and sits right by her side. Mrs. Mathews gets up from her chair and tells everyone that she has to go to the bathroom but she will be right back. Mr. Mathews gets up and says " Yvonne I will go with you wait for me." The Mathews walk out of the room and Karen tells Rodney " how are you, and why am I here Rodney?" Rodney replies back with a kiss on Karen's forehead and tries to get ready to explain the car accident but a Dr. comes in and says hello Karen....You are a very lucky woman." You have just survived a bad car accident. How are you feeling right now? Karen looks at Rodney and responds back very confidently " well I am feeling just fine, is there anything wrong." The Dr. replies back and says "oh no Karen you look pretty good actually and your tests results came back negative but I want to monitor you for a day then you can go home. You had a huge gash on the side of your head. Karen eyes begin get big and she lifts her right hand in the air and tries to touch the right side of her head and began to start feeling for the gash. Karen's gash on her head was wrapped in white cloth that was tied around her head. The Dr. asks Karen if she needs anything and prescribes some pain medicine for Karen to take in the next 4 hours. Karen agrees to take them and then the Dr. takes a look at Karen and Rodney and smiles and says, you are a lucky man. I will be in touch, get some rest Karen and I will see you all in the morning. Karen begins to get sleepy again so she lays her head on Rodney's chest and Rodney lays his head back onto the pillows and drifts off to sleep. The Mathews come into the room quietly and turn on the TV and began to eat their takeout dinner. The nurse comes in the room and asks how many will be staying the night and Mr. Mathews stated that they will only need one bed for Rodney and that they will be back in the morning. The nurse nodded and agrees and leaves the room and comes right back and wheels a bed into the room for Rodney. The nurse sets up the bed and then asks again if they needed anything. The Mathews reply back and says no, no thank you. The nurse smiles back at the Mathews and walks out of the room. The Mathews look at each other and smile and each other reaches out for one another to hold. The Mathews embrace each other and console each other. Rodney's friend JT knocks on the door and Rodney awakes by the knock at the door and Rodney motions for JT to come into the room. Mr. and Mrs. Mathews sit up straight in their chair while saying hello to JT's entrance into the room. Rodney introduces JT to Karen who is still asleep and to her parents. The Mathews nod back and stand up and announce that they will be going and that they will be back first thing in the morning. The Mathews walk over to Karen's bed and gives her a kiss on her cheek while Rodney steps down off the bed to stand and wish the Mathews a good night. The Mathews begin to walk out the room and JT tells them good night to and that he was honored to meet them. The Mathews reply back and says " like- wise, see you all in the morning" Mr. Mathews replies back to Rodney and says get some rest Rodney, you are going to need it. The door shuts and JT and Rodney sits down in the chairs and JT begins to say to Rodney that he could not find the man that Rodney described to him in the hospital, but he did hear the word on the streets that the Brinkley's of the "Brinkley's Oil and Gas Company put a hit out on Karen." Rodney's mouth drop open and says "man you are kidding me?" JT replies back and says " man would I lie to you? I am serious and that is not all I found out either. There is someone on the inside of Karen's company who is working directly for the Brinkley's. Rodney puts his hand over his mouth and says man thank you, I don't know what I would do without you. JT replies back and says you better call your people and let her parents know fast. You never know what will happen next around here. JT reaches into his jacket and pulls out a gun and tells him that he needs to keep this on him at all times. The mafia is no joke and they will keep coming after you until they know you are dead, but I don't think you got any worries. The hit out is just after Karen. In the meantime put the gun away and make sure no one sees it on you. If you can lock this door tonight lock it but if not try to have a policeman sitting outside of Karen's door to help keep her safe. JT gets up from talking with Rodney and hugs him and says I love you man and remember do what you have to do to keep Karen safe. Rodney replies back fo sho, man I got this. JT walks out the room and looks to the left and to the right and a policeman is sitting down directly across from Karen's Room. JT smiles and nodes to the police officer with respect who is on duty for Karen and then walks away. Rodney puts the gun away and climbs back into the bed with Karen and pulls the blankets up over the both of them and reaches over and kisses Karen on the nose and then Karen smiles in her sleep and Rodney lays his head back onto the pillows and closes his eyes and then drifts off.

Chapter 6
Still Standing

Karen begins to wake up and notices that she is in the inside of her house in her bedroom. Karen looks all around her room and notices that she is wearing a set of her favorite silk pajamas. Vicky is sitting next to her in a chair. Vicky gets up and walks over to Karen and says "hello beautiful." Karen replies back and says hello back. Karen tries to get up on her own but falls back down on the bed. Vicky starts to laugh and says to Karen come on you are going to be okay. Karen tries to get up again and Vicky extends her hand out to help Karen up and out of the bed. Karen steps down from her step stool that's connected to the queen size high leveled bed and walks into the bathroom. Karen turns on the light and glances at herself in the mirror looks for the white wrap that was wrapped around her head from the hospital. Karen keeps walking to the bathroom. Karen goes inside then pulls her pants down and sits down on the bathroom seat and hears a loud sound that sounds like a shot gun. Vicky runs into the bathroom and tells Karen to hurry up that they have to go and not to make a sound. Karen does exactly what Vicky tells her to do and Karen motions to let her know that she to get her shoes and that there is a secret place for them if Vicky will follow her. Karen and Vicky here men voices down stairs and Karen and Vicky run into Karen's closet and Karen pushes a button and the door opens and Vicky and Karen step inside and then the door shuts quality back. Vicky whispers to Karen and says does anyone else know about this secret hiding place Karen? Karen shakes her head and says no. Vicky nods back at Karen and takes a deep breath and sighs. Karen begins to search for the remote control to turn on the cameras downstairs in her house.

Vicky's mouth drops open and comes over to sit by Karen and sits down by Karen to get a clear photo of who is in Karen's house down stairs. Karen and Vicky both hear two men talking with heavy accents. Karen is trying to make out their voices but she can't. One of the men says she is not here....and the other man replies back and says she has got to be here somewhere. Karen covers her mouth to keep any noise from getting out and Vicky begins to start praying that the two men do not find them and that they leave. One of the men with a thick heavy accent blurts out and says to the other man to "call and tell Baldwin that we can't find her anywhere." The man dials Baldwin's number and Baldwin answers the phone and says" did you find her yet? One of the men replies back and says no boss, we have not found Karen yet, but we will keep looking for her. Karen's eyes get big and begin to try to get a full image of the two men in her closet from the hidden cameras in her ceiling light fixture. The women are able to get a good description of the two men wearing all black clothing. Vicky is shocked by she just heard and at the fact that Baldwin has something to do with Karen's hit from the mafia. The two men leave the room walk back down the steps holding up their guns in mid- air. Karen watches the men get into their car and drive off. Karen looks over at Vicky who has just passed out from seeing everything that just happened. Karen begins to calm herself down and pushes herself to get dressed. Karen locates plenty of extra clothes she can pick from and grabs a wig that will help transform into another woman. Vicky suddenly begins to wake up and stare at Karen and blinks twice and looks stunned. Karen tells Vicky that it's all right but she can no longer look like the old Karen right now. Karen also tells Vicky that she strongly advises her to do the same thing. Vicky replies back and says well I guess I have no choice when there is a billion dollars at risk. Karen smiles and looks over at Vicky and tells her " Showtime. Lights, Camera and Money! " Karen now believes that the reason people are after her is because of her oil and money she owns. Vicky replies back and says " why couldn't you just marry someone with a lot of money. Karen smiles back and says why, when I got my own money. Vicky replies back and says " I know this is completely off the conversation but have you ever heard back from that woods guy, you know who I am talking about don't you? Karen smiles and says oh you are talking about that Anthony woods guy, who is a friend of Brian and Keisha. Vicky replies back as she is almost putting on all her clothes and says " well I was always told that a woman can see how much money a man has by his watch and by his shoes that he wears. Karen laughs and says Vicky where did you get that from? Vicky replies back and says to Karen "tell the truth and shame the devil." Karen replies back and says "Amen" Vicky goes on to say 'thank you Lord right now for all your blessings and for all your benefits and we pray that you keep us safe." Karen shouts out "Glory"...Glory to God and all his benefits." Vicky walks over to Karen and start waving a handkerchief over her." Karen replies back and says " If God is for us then who can be against us." Vicky replies back and says Amen." Karen opens up her eyes and sits down on the floor and says "what am I going to do and what am I going to say to him? Karen says "what am I going to tell Rodney? Vicky says to Karen "see no evil...hear no evil." Karen replies back and says to Vicky "preach...this is gospel." The two women laugh and begin to put on their shoes. Karen tells Vicky that she has a special door passage way that leads to the next house, which is also her house too, but she has people staying in it for the time being. Karen begins to also tell her that there is a car that has tinted windows on it and that they will need to take that car to get out of here. Vicky gives Karen a hug and tells her that she is proud of her and that she loves her and that she will make it past this. Karen smiles and says " I know that I will, I know what type of God I serve." The women begin to go through the special passage door that will lead them to the neighbors next door. Karen is walking really fast and Vicky is trying to keep up with Karen. Karen yells back you have to keep up Vicky. Vicky yells okay, I am sorry Karen but it's really dark in some places down here. Karen says be quite because she hears something. Karen hears a noise directly above their heads. Karen and Vicky are listening and realize that it must be the mail man's truck that keeps stopping and going every few feet. Karen tells Vicky that she must stay close to her and that she does not have long to go. The women finally get to where they were trying to go and Karen turns the knob to open the door and the room is already lit up and has just as much as Karen's other hide out place was. Karen grabs the hidden keys and begins to stuff them in her mouth and tells Vicky to put these certain shades on Vicky nodded her head and reaches for the sunglasses to put on and puts them on. Karen begins to walk up a ladder and Vicky follows her up the ladder which brings them to a hidden garage where there is a car covered with a gray tarp to protect the car. Karen runs over to the car and begin to take off the tarp. Vicky begins to help Karen with the tarp and then Karen tells Vicky to get into the car. Karen opens the driver side door and gets in and turns on the car and then puts the car in reverse and then backs out of the drive way. Vicky begins to ask questions about where they are going. Karen tells her that they are going over to her mom's house and that she needs to not make any phone calls and to make sure her cell phone is turned off so no one can trace them. Vicky says okay and sits back and puts her seat belt on. The women arrive at Karen's mother's house. The guard Jameson lets them in. Karen drives to the back of the house. While driving Karen is looking for extra cars and people that she does not know. Karen parks the car and tells Vicky to get out and Karen gets out of the car and walks over to the back door of her parents' house. The door is open and Karen finds her father and mother sitting at the table. Karen rushes over to her father and mother and tells them what happened and then the Mathews get up and walk up stairs to their bedroom and Karen and Vicky begin to follow them up stairs. Mr. Mathews tells Mrs. Mathews that he was afraid that the Baldwin could be in on something with the Brinkley's. The Mathews' are walking around their room thought things that they think that they will need into their bags. Mr. Mathews tells everyone that she is ready and the shortly after Mr. Mathews tells everyone too that he is packed and ready to go. Everyone begins to walk down the stairs and Mr. Mathews cell phone rings and he answers the phone and his mother Mrs. Naomi Wellington-Mathews says that she is right outside and that she is sorry that she is late and if someone can come and open up the door for her. Mr. Mathews says " yes mother, I am on my way to open the door. Mrs. Mathews looks at Mr. Mathews and says I didn't know that she was coming over today. Mr. Mathews replies back and says I did not know either. Mr. Mathews walks over to the door and lets his mother inside the house. Mr. Mathew's mother looks over at Karen and says hello to her and walks over to give her a hug. Mr. Mathews says hello mother what brings you by today? Naomi replies back and says "oh I was in the area and I thought I might just come by and say hello plus I happen to see Karen use the secret tunnel to get here. Karen's mouth dropped open and Vicky eyes gets big and Mrs. Mathews look over at her husband. Naomi looks at Mr. Mathews and says " Does someone want to tell me what is going on? Karen begins to tell Naomi what is going on and Naomi reaches over to hug Karen again and says " I am sorry love if only I had known all of this would be happening…I would of…I would of never married Mr. Mathews. Karen looks at her grandmother and says oh no. It's not your fault. Naomi looks Mr. Mathews straight in the eyes and says my family will do no more fighting or running. Today we will go and see the Brinkley's. I have a thing or two to say to Yvonne Brinkley. Everyone looks at each other and drops their bags and says that they will all drive together over to the Brinkley's estate. The family all prepare to walk outside and get into the car and go over to the Brinkley's house. Mr. Mathews is the last one to leave and lock up. Mr. Mathews begins to put the SUV in reverse and backs out of the driveway. The Mathews make it over to the Brinkley's house and Mr. and Mrs. Brinkley's car is at home. The guard lets them through the gate. Mr. Mathews pulls the SUV up to the front gated French double tower doors trimmed with real gold. The Mathew's get out of the car and walk up the steps to get to the front door and the Brinkley's butler opens the door and lets them in. The butler tells them to wait here while he gets Mr. and Mrs. Brinkley. Naomi blurts out and says "wow I can't remember when was the last time I was here at this house. It has to have been over 50 years ago now since I used to date Yvonne's Father Mr. Brinkley. Karen's mouths drop open and says "grandma did you just say that you used to date Mr. Brinkley?" Mr. Brinkley and Mrs. Brinkley step into the room and says " oh yes Karen my father loved your grandmother very much so." Naomi smiles and look over at Mr. Brinkley and says " you look just like your father, and you don't look a day over 50. Mrs. Brinkley looks at Mrs. Mathews and Karen and says "wow what do we have the honor to have you all here in our home today?" Naomi walks over to Mrs. Brinkley and says your evil plans concerning my granddaughter and my family will end today and if not I will pull everything you have, after all your oil is really my oil and my land. Everything was willed to me when Mr. Brinkley passed away. Mrs. Brinkley looks at Mr. Brinkley and says " is this true?" Mr. Brinkley bows his head down and looks down at the floor and says yes, Yvonne this is true Mrs. Mathews has been so gracious that she allowed us to keep our part of my father's oil rights, which she still controls till this very day. Mrs. Mathews looks at her husband and her husband is shocked that his mother has the final say so about the Brinkley's Oil and Gas this whole entire time. Mrs. Brinkley closes her mouth and looks at everyone in the room and then dismisses herself from the meeting they were having. Naomi looks over at Mr. Brinkley and says make sure that I don't hear of your wife trying to harm my family again or I will take everything from you and leave you with nothing but the shirt on your back. This is my family and I will protect it any cause. Mr. Brinkley replies back and says " you have my word Mrs. Mathews." Mr. Mathews looks at Mr. Brinkley and says now how do we work from here? Mr. Brinkley tells Mr. Mathews that they will set up a board meeting on Monday for the families to get together and work. Mr. Brinkley shakes Mr. Mathews hand and then Mrs. Mathews says and please call off the hit for my daughter Karen please. The Mathews began to walk out of the Brinkley's house and walk down the steps and Carolyn Brinkley looks at the Mathews up and down and says what are you guys doing here...where is my mother. Naomi stops walking down the steps and says go and ask your mother dear and if I ever hear of you or your family trying to kill my family again I will take you out. Carolyn eyes gets big and Carolyn gets stuck and can't move, so she just stands there and watches the Mathews get back into their car and drive off. Mrs. Brinkley walks outside and greets her daughter Carolyn on the steps and says don't worry they have not seen or heard the last of us.

Chapter 7
The Best for Last

Keisha is at home watching TV, waiting for Brian to get home. Suddenly Keisha remembers that Brian's friend Anthony has the big ball tonight. Keisha jumps off the sofa and nearly falls across the coffee table. Keisha breaks her fall by putting one hand on the table and while balancing her other hand in the air. Slowly she pulls herself together and sits back down on the sofa and takes a deep breath. Karen pulls up into Keisha's driveway and parks the car and gets out of the car and walks over to Keisha's window and peeps in and sees Keisha sitting on the sofa as usual. Keisha looks at her watch and thinks to herself hmm....Brian is off of work early today. Keisha walks over to the door and sees Karen and opens the door. Keisha screams "hello Karen" and takes a step forward to hug Karen and says girl I have missed you. Karen smiles to herself and exhale. The women walk through the hallway of Keisha's house. Keisha looks over at Karen and tells Karen "don't break nothing this time and whatever you do, don't faint." The women began to laugh and sit down on the sofa together. Keisha says to Karen "girl you are looking good; whatever you are using, I want some." Karen replies back....It's called peace. The women both laugh together and hit high five. Karen then takes a look at Keisha and tells her that she too looks amazing and that she is also glowing. Keisha looks down and off to the side and tries not to blush while smiling. Keisha blurts out what are you going to wear Karen? We have the ball tonight with Anthony Woods....Your better half Karen. Karen looks stunned and says "Oh my gosh!" "Keisha, the ball is tonight. What am I going to wear? Better yet, what am I going to tell Rodney?" Keisha replies back and says "well I see that you didn't remember, so take a look at the address on the tickets." "The address is of the River Oaks Hotel located here in Atlanta, GA." Oh that reminds me Anthony had stopped by our house and left a message for me to give to you Karen and here it is. Thank you, Keisha. Keisha looks at Karen and says "well go ahead and read it, don't be shy." Karen reads out loud what Anthony wrote to her. Dear Karen, I hope this letter finds you in time for the ball. It would mean a lot to me if you all would come and be my special guest. Karen's eyes get big and then she looks over at Keisha and covers her mouth, while trying to compose herself, while finish reading Anthony's letter. "I will be at the Alexander's home at 6:00 p.m. to pick you and the Alexander's up in my private limo. "I wish to see you soon and I look forward in talking and hearing from you." Karen blushes and falls backwards into Keisha's sofa and says "I like this man." Keisha replies back to Karen and says "well you should, he is a good man and I like him for you already." Speaking of good men, where is Rodney at?" "You know he can't be good for nothing." Karen tries not to laugh and says "I believe he has a game out of state tonight." "Rodney offered to fly me to the game, but I told him that I would just sit this one out and watch him on TV." Keisha looks at Karen with a serious look on her face and says "what are you going to do?" "Do you have a dress?" Karen replies back and says "no but I will ask Emma to go and pick me out." "I need to focus on this hair." Keisha reaches over and touches Karen's hair and say's "ouch, you can say that again." Karen grabs a pillow and hits Keisha with the pillow and the women laugh together. Keisha looks at Karen and says "well." Karen looks at Keisha and says "well. what Mrs. I got it all Keisha?" Keisha looks Karen right in her eyes and says to Karen "are you not going to call this man or not?" Karen looks at Keisha and says "oh yeah you are right, I guess I should call him right now and thank him." Keisha looks at Karen and says' ah yeah you think, Karen you need to call him right now before it gets any later." Karen grabs her cell phone out of her purse and calls Anthony. The phone is rings and Anthony picks up on the second ring and says " hello" Karen replies back and says "hello, ah this is Karen, Karen Mathews." " I met you a couple of days ago at my friend's house ah the Alexander's." Anthony replies back and says " awe yes, how can I forget someone as beautiful as you." Karen begins to blush and smiles into the phone. Keisha can't help but to play Karen's words back to her, while she is still on the phone with Anthony. Karen's eyes gets big and then puts her focus back onto what Anthon was saying and tries to rush the conversation to end. Karen looks at Keisha and puts her finger over her lips to try to tell Keisha to be quiet. Anthony is still talking and Karen just decides to sit down while trying to be attentive to what Anthony is saying. Keisha just looks at Karen smiles. Karen suddenly tries to clear up the smile on her face and replies back and says "awe thank you, you are handsome yourself." Anthony replies back and says "Karen thank you for calling me." " I almost was afraid that you were not going to be able to make it to the ball tonight." "Karen you will be there tonight won't you? Karen replies back and says "yes, yes Anthony I will be coming tonight." Anthony says' okay great I will be there to pick you up. Karen thank you again for calling me and I can't wait to see you again." Karen blushes again with butterflies in stomach this time and says " likewise Anthony. I shall see you again soon." Karen pushes end button on the cell phone and then touches her stomach and says to Keisha " Anthony gives me butterflies...Oh My Gosh Keisha." Keisha smiles and says "I remember when Brian and I first met and I would get them all the time." Karen looks at Keisha and into her eyes and says "you two are the cutest couple I know." Keisha jumps up and says enough about me and Brian, you got to go and get something done to that hair of yours. Keisha jumps up too and says " just wait I am going to look fine as wine. Just you wait." Keisha says well you better get a head start on it now so you can look " fine as wine." Both women began to laugh and hug each other once more. Karen begins to look for her coat and purse. Keisha walks over to Karen to give her, her things so she can go. Keisha walks Karen to the front door and they both say goodbye to each other. Karen walks off and gets into her car and Keisha lays her head gently on the door while waiting for Karen to speeds off. Keisha smiles while closing her eyes and says "yes, she is finally happy... this is the one for her. Thank you. Lord!" Rodney pulls up into Karen's driveway trying to surprise her. Rodney decides that he wants to go ahead and come into Karen's house and sits himself down on her couch and makes his self at home. Rodney looks around and gets his cell phone out and calls

Karen and Karen answers her phone and says" Hello." Rodney asks Karen where she is at the moment and Karen replies back and says "I am on my way to get my hair done and then I will be home, why? Where are you at Rodney? I am sitting inside your house. Karen can't help keep the dead silence that breaks into their conversation and Karen tries to keep talking but she is stunned on how Rodney was able to get inside of her house without trying to sound offensive, she fails and blurts out "Rodney how did you get into my house. Rodney says hello Karen are you there, I can't hear you, I am sorry it must be a bad connection. Karen yells out loud Rodney I am still here can you hear me. Rodney replies back and says that he thought he almost thought he lost her. Karen can you repeat what you were trying to say again I couldn't hear you. Karen replies back and says how did you get into to my house? Rodney replies back and says do you not remember where you always put my extra spare key outside your door in the flower pot. Karen replies back yes I remember that. Rodney grabs Karen's jacket and smells her jacket to see is he can smell her perfume left on her jacket. Karen replies back and says well I' m sorry I am not home right now and I honestly don't know when I will be ready because you know how my stylist is. Don't wait up for me. I hope you have a good game and I wish you safe travels sweetheart. Rodney replies back and says okay well I just wanted to see you before the game. I have to get ready to go to the airport any way love. Karen replies back and says good luck on the game and I will see you when you get back in tomorrow. Karen hangs up the phone and then Rodney removes the phone from his face and looks at the phone and is shocked that he did not get a chance to say good bye. Rodney takes another swift of Karen's jacket and begins to sing " Beautiful Girl…..Beautiful Girl I' think I've found an angel" and he begins to dance and twirls around and walks out the door and locks Karen's front door and put the extra key back into the soil in the flower pot. Karen begins to sigh and smile while she is driving and pulls into the hair salon. Karen gets out of the car and walks into the salon and tells her hairstylist that she needs something special because she is going to a ball tonight. Karen's stylist smiles and tells her " honey child you are going to look wonderful. Come on and sit yourself down." Karen's hair stylist begins to style Karen's hair. Karen closes her eyes and the hair stylist puts some music on to help relax her and he begins to shampoo her hair. Karen falls asleep underneath the dryer and is wakened up by the other guest who comes into the salon to get their hair done and she thinks she hears Keisha friend named Jasmine. Karen over hears Jasmine talk about her NBA basketball player fiancé named Rodney. Karen almost jumps out of her seat but remembers that she can't because the hair stylist is doing her hair and that he has hot curling irons in her hair. Karen tries to humble herself to listen Jasmine talk about her having a special party for all of their friends. Karen begins to cry and her stylist asks if she is okay and Karen replies back and says " I'm okay I am just allergic to cheap perfume." Karen's hairstylist Russell says ooh girl I thought it was just me but you smell it too on that girl all the way down there. Karen and her stylist begin to laugh and he tells Karen well I do have to say myself that you look stunning. Girl, honey whoever he is your man is going to fall head over heels in love with you tonight. You look simply beautiful. Karen smiles and gets up and looks in the mirror and says you are amazing Russell. Thank you so much. How much do I owe you, nothing beautiful just go out and have the time of your life. Karen tips her hair stylist and walks out the door and shuts the door and walks back to her car and unlocks it. Karen looks up at the ceiling in her car and begins to talk to Jesus and says "Jesus I need a word from you!" Lord, please show me the man you want in my life and I to marry. Karen starts her engine and puts her car in reverse and backs out and drives home and pulls up and sees a man carrying red roses from her front door and she parks her car and gets out and tries to stop the flower man. The flower man stops and turns around and smiles and says wow you look beautiful. Whoever he is, he is a lucky man. Here these roses are for you. Karen smiles and says to the flower man thank you and takes a sniff of the roses as she closes her eyes and smiles. The flower delivery man tells her that there is a note inside of the roses. Karen thanks the man and opens the note in the roses and it's a note from Anthony saying " Dear Karen" I hope you didn't mind me getting your address from your friend Keisha. I wanted to thank you for this opportunity to spend time with you tonight. I can't wait to see you and I look forward in talking and seeing you tonight. Karen is blown away by the sweet gesture of roses. Karen begins to walk toward the house and then turns around and sees Emma pull up in the drive and park. Karen waits for Emma to get out the car and walk over to her. Emma is so excited about the dress she finds for Karen and how Karen looks with the new hair style. Emma asks Karen who the roses are from. Karen replies back and says they are from her new date tonight Anthony woods. Emma looks Karen and smiles and says what are you waiting for...We can't keep this man waiting let's get you dressed and all dolled up. Karen and Emma walk into the house and Emma tells Karen to go upstairs so she can try on the gown that she just picked out for her. Karen is so excited about tonight and she goes upstairs Emma follows her up stairs to her bedroom. Karen's phone starts ringing and Karen answers the phone and says " hello" Keisha replies back on the other line and says hey beautiful how is everything coming along. Karen replies back and says everything is going great. Keisha replies back and says okay great I can't wait to see you within the next hour and a half. Karen's eyes gets big and says Oh! my gosh okay Keisha okay I got to go so I can get fitted for my dress and take my shower. Keisha replies back and says okay beautiful see you in just a bit. Emma grabs the cell phone out of Karen's hand and tells Karen to take off her clothes so she can help her put the dress on. Karen begins to take off her clothes to step into the dress that Emma picked out. Karen puts on the dress and Emma tells Karen to turn around and see herself in the mirror. A tear runs down Emma's face and says you look so beautiful Karen and I hope you have a great time tonight with Anthony. Karen hugs Emma and says I believe I will have the time of my life. Emma tells Karen to hurry to get out of her dress so she can shower and be on time for the ball tonight. Karen steps out of the dress and walks into the bathroom and shuts the door and begins to start the shower. Emma bangs on the door and says no....no Karen don't get in the shower yet until she wraps her hair. Karen yells out thank you Emma. Karen comes out of the bathroom all dolled up and ready to step into her dress and she puts her favorite perfume on and then slips on her dress and then her shoes and then Emma stands and stays you look beautiful let me zip you up in the back. Karen looks at herself one more time and then grabs her purse and then walks down the steps to walk out the door and Emma follows her out the door and watches Karen get into the car. Karen starts the car and puts the car into reverse and backs out into the street and slowly drives off and begins to hum to herself. Karen finds herself over at Keisha's house sooner than what she expected. Karen pulls up to Keisha's house and gets out the car while grabbing with one hand her cream vintage lace dress. Karen walks up to Keisha 's door and knocks on the door and Keisha's comes to answer the door and Keisha stands back in awe and tells Karen that she looks stunning. Karen walks into the house and tells Keisha that she looks beautiful too and Keisha replies back and says thank you. Brian walks down the steps and he tells the two lovely women that they look very beautiful and that Anthony just called him and told him that he is just around the corner. Karen smiles and looks a little nervous. Keisha looks over at Karen and tells her just to remember to be calm and to be herself. Karen replies back and says "well Keisha that all I know how to do." Keisha smiles at Karen and then the doorbell rings and it is Anthony at the door. Karen is blown away when Anthony walks into the living room wearing an all-black and white tuxedo. Karen begins to get butterflies again and begins to blush. Anthony greets Keisha and Brian and then walks over to Karen and reaches out for Karen's hand and says" May I kiss your hand?" Karen replies back with a nod as Anthony bends down to kiss her hand. Karen, I hope you don't mind but I got something special for you. Can you close your eyes and Karen replies back and says yes and Anthony walks in back of Karen pulls a necklace out of his suit coat pocket and takes out a five diamond karat platinum necklace out and places it around Karen's neck. Karen is stunned by Anthony's kind gesture. Anthony asks Karen if she liked the necklace and Karen looks down at her necklace and begins to smile and says yes, yes thank you Anthony. Anthony looks at Karen and asks if she is ready to go to the ball and asks her would she do the honors of escorting him to the ball and Karen answers back and says "yes." Brian then grabs Keisha's hand and asks Keisha if she would do him the honor of escorting him to the ball. Keisha replies back and says "yes, of course." The couple began to walk out of the house one by one and step into the white Rose Royce trimmed in gold limo. Brian stops walking and pauses for a moment and takes his focus off of Keisha. Keisha notices that Brian's attention is not only on her but he also stops walking towards the limo. Brian turns his head and glances up the street and sees an all black limo down the street. The limo looks out of place Brian thinks to his self and then he turns his head back to focus on Keisha. Brian then looks at everyone around him and then back at the limo. Brian tries to smile carelessly and looks back at Keisha and drops her hand and tells Keisha to watch her step. Keisha begins to take a step and get into the limo and sits down. Brian turns his head again to see if he notices the other again that is black and trimmed in gold. The black limo is still sitting still from a distance. The black limo driver flashes his lights towards Brian. Brian takes a look around and he can't see anyone else standing outside. Only Brian and his friends are standing outside. Brian turns his focus back onto the black limo and tries to sequent his eyes to see who's driving the limo. The windows are tinted too dark for Brian to see who the driver is. The limo begins to take off and drive very slow down towards Brian and Keisha's street. Brian tells Karen to quickly get into the limo, so they all don't be late going to the ball. Anthony notices that Brian is in a rush to get to the ball and thanks' Brian for coming to support him and his company tonight. Brian rushes to step into the limo and sit down and puts on his seatbelt and say's awe man any time. Anthony tells the limo driver to drive on. Keisha notices the quick change in Brian and asks if he is alright. Brian replies back and says "Yes, Yes Keisha I' am okay, just ready to get this night started. '' Keisha smiles and grabs for Brian's hand to hold. Brian puts his hand into Keisha's hand. Keisha knows that there is something wrong, but she doesn't know what. Brian looks back at Keisha's face then turns his head and tries to figure out what just happened. Keisha looks back at Brian in disbelief. The all black Limo trimmed in gold begins to pick up speed and tries to drive into Anthony's limo. Anthony's limo driver Adam honks his horn three times to alert the other limo driver. The all black limo just barely missed hitting Anthony's limo on the left side where Anthony was sitting at. Adam Anthony's limo driver rolls his window down and yells out ''Hey watch where you are going you creep, you could of killed us all.'' Anthony's limo driver rolls his window back up and then rolls his window down on the inside of the limo and asks if everyone is okay. Adam then tries to apologies for the other limo drivers driving. Anthony looks up and say's ''Oh it's okay Adam it's not your fault, you can't control someone else's driving.'' Adam says back to Anthony '' you right about that boss.'' Anthony then looks around at everyone and asks if they are alright? Everyone but Keisha replies back and says that they are ok. Keisha takes a deep breath then pauses for a moment to gain her composure without trying to letting everyone see her face. Keisha looks at Brian and then takes a look around to make sure everyone is okay. Karen takes her seat belt off and rises up and turns around to see if she can get a glimpse of the license plate on the other limo. Karen can't see the license plate, so she turns back around and puts her seat belt. Keisha reaches for Brian's hand. Anthony grabs Karen's hand and then puts his left arm around Karen to comfort her. Brian looks over at Keisha and then motions to Keisha to move closer to him so they can be closer to each other for the rest of the ride. Brian sighs then lays his head back and against the leather interior seats and closes his eyes. Keisha looks at Karen and then mouths to Karen without speaking and says that they needed to talk. Karen nodded her head in agreement with Keisha's request. Karen then turns and looks away and closes her eyes. Keisha turns and looks up at Brian, then she began to lay her head into Brian's chest and tries to get comfortable to enjoy the ride to the ball. Adam looks around at everyone and notices everyone's reactions while sitting in the back seats. Adam sees that no one is paying attention, so he grabs for his cell phone to make a call ,then pushes the button to roll up the inside window to the guest and makes a phone call. Everyone arrives shortly after to the ball. Adam gets out of the call and Anthony tells everyone that they are there. Karen reaches for her purse and Anthony gets up and tries to open up the door. Adam opens up the door and Anthony steps out of the limo and Adam greets Anthony with a smile. Anthony extends his hand out towards Karen to help her get out of the limo. Keisha stays seated to allow Brian to step out of the limo first, while he extends his hand to help Keisha get out of the limo. Brian and Keisha both tell Adam thank you. Adam shuts the door to the limo door then smiles again and stands in front of the limo door. Adam looks at everyone says ''you all are blessed to see another day, enjoy your night out.'' Everyone's looks shocked by Adam's statement and didn't know what to say, so they all began to walk off towards the ball. Anthony reaches out to give Adam a hi -five and tells Adam '' Thank you for everything man.'' Adam tells Anthony '' have a good night with Karen, man you deserve it.'' Anthony smiles right back at Adam and says ''Man she is the one… I just know it.'' Anthony turns around and begins to walks off into the same direction of the Hollywood spot lights and disappears. Adam feels his cell is about to go off and vibrate, so he looks around and sees only a couple of people standing around talking and laughing. Adam doesn't see anyone that he knows so he grabs his cell phone from his pocket and struggles to grab his cell phone out of his pocket. Before anyone could hear his phone go off again or had the chance to stop and pay attention Adam opens up his car door and sits in the driver's seat. Adam says ''hello 'to the familiar voice on the phone. The mysterious voice replies back and says ''You're late'' Adam shrugs his shoulders and replies back and says '' I know…I know, I am sorry. I am on my way. Everyone just left the limo.'' The person on the other line hangs up without notice. Adam hangs up his cell phone and places it in the passenger seat and then rubs his hands through his hair and then starts the ignition and puts the limo in gear and then takes a deep breath and looks around then drives off.

About The Author

Aneesah S. Perkins was born and raised in Edmond, Oklahoma. Aneesah graduated from *Langston University* with a Bachelor's Degree in Education, with a minor in Architecture while studying extensively at the *University of Texas at Arlington.*

While attending college, Aneesah opened her first business at the age of twenty-two as a florist, wedding planner, and designer. Perkins's first business was named *"Byron Blake's Floral Designs. "* It was later upgraded, to *"The Garden of Eden Boutique & Spa."* Aneesah was certified by *Tela Flora* and became the first Two -day wedding planner in the state of Oklahoma as the first *Native American* woman to have a *French Style Luxury Boutique & Spa* in Oklahoma City, Oklahoma. Inspiration flourished and Aneesah Perkins created *"Mahogany Brides Magazine U.S."* in 2011 and launched the magazine January 1, 2012 for Brides and Grooms. Mahogany Brides Magazine U.S. inspired her to create a television show called *"Mahogany Bride and Groom Weddings*, "which is due to air October *2013.*

Poetry and art inspired her to write plays, movies, and books. Aneesah, An author, who writes her own experiences as a single woman, and a married woman with three children. Faith was taught at an early age. Later she converted from the *Muslim* religion to *Christianity*. It was then, that she fully understood how to "...walk by faith and not by sight." (2 Corinthians 5:7 KJV) It was from this *"WOW" Walking on Waters Productions* was created in 2013 but established in 2016. *"LOVE BANK"* is her first stage play, book, TV Show and movie. The book will be released on *October 1, 2013.* "LOVE

BANK," the movie is scheduled to be released in 2017.

A woman of many talents... Author Aneesah Perkins does not only love to design and create furniture, but also loves to empower men, women and youth. By second nature Spring of 2014 Aneesah Perkins stepped out on faith, and created her own signature bridal, Tuxedo and couture clothing line. As a great but up and coming designer; Perkins wanted to help others and herself in the fashion industry. With a great plan in mind and handpicked board members she created the Oklahoma Chamber of Fashion Designers and the Dallas Chamber of Fashion Designers and fashion incubator. Her latest work is the "Dallas International Fashion Festival" week (Fall 2014).

Love Bank's TV Series and Movie 2017

Coming Soon!

Thank You. **LOVE** BANK Fans!

Love Bank II will be available to purchase on June 1, 2015. Thank you for supporting Love Bank. Love Bank can be purchased online at www.lovebank.weebly.com or at Amazon, Barnes & Noble or Lulu.